English Verbs

with

101 Videos for Your iPod

Rory Ryder

Illustrated by Andy Garnica

Mc Graw Hill

New York   Chicago   San Francisco   Lisbon   London   Madrid   Mexico City
Milan   New Delhi   San Juan   Seoul   Singapore   Sydney   Toronto

1 2 3 4 5 6 7 8 9 10 11 12 13 14 15 16 17 18 19 20 21 22 23 24   CTPS/CTPS   0 9

ISBN 978-0-07-161580-8 (book and disk set)
MHID   0-07-161580-6

ISBN 978-0-07-161581-5 (book alone)
MHID   0-07-161581-4

Library of Congress Control Number: 2008935418

Illustrated by Andy Garnica

McGraw-Hill books are available at special quantity discounts to use as premiums and sales promotions or for use in corporate training programs. To contact a representative, please e-mail us at bulksales@mcgraw-hill.com.

Also in this series:
101 French Verbs with 101 Videos for Your iPod
101 Japanese Verbs with 101 Videos for Your iPod
101 Spanish Verbs with 101 Videos for Your iPod
101 English Verbs: The Art of Conjugation
101 French Verbs: The Art of Conjugation
101 German Verbs: The Art of Conjugation
101 Italian Verbs: The Art of Conjugation
101 Spanish Verbs: The Art of Conjugation

Also available:
Verbots Illustrated Verbs interactive Whiteboard materials from Promethean
For more information, please visit PrometheanWorld.com/learnverbs

Contents

How to Use This Book   iv

Verb Conjugation in English   vi

Verb Tenses   viii

Present Simple   viii

Present Continuous   ix

Past Continuous   x

Past Simple   xi

Future   xii

Conditional   xiii

Present Perfect   xiv

Command   xv

Gerund   xv

Reflexive Verbs   xvi

Phrasal Verbs   xvii

The Passive   xviii

101 English Verb Conjugations   1

Verb Index   102

The Passive Construction   109

Regular Verb Conjugation   110

How to Use This Book

When learning a language, we often have problems remembering the words; it does not mean we have totally forgotten them. It just means that we can't recall them at that particular moment. This book is designed to help learners recall the verbs and their conjugations instantly.

Research

Research has shown that one of the most effective ways to remember something is by association. In this book, the verb (or keyword) has been included in each illustration, which acts as a means to stimulate long-term memory. This method is seven times more effective than passively reading and responding to a list of verbs.

New Approach

Most grammar and verb books relegate the vital task of learning verbs to a black-and-white world of bewildering tables, leaving the student bored and frustrated. *101 English Verbs* is committed to clarifying the importance of this process through stimulating the senses, not by dulling them.

Dynamic Illustrations and Videos

The illustrations and videos introduce the quirky world of the Verbots in an approach that goes beyond conventional verb books. To make the most of this book, spend time with each picture and video to become familiar with everything that is happening. These images present mini storylines and episodes. Some are more challenging than others, adding to the fun but, more important, aiding the memory process.

Keywords

We have called the infinitive the "keyword" to refer to its central importance in remembering the multiple ways it can be used. Once you have located the keyword and made the connection with the illustration, you are ready to start to learn the colo(u)r-coded tenses.

Colo(u)r-Coded Verb Tables

The verb tables are designed to save learners valuable time by focusing their attention and allowing them to make immediate connections between the subject and the verb. Making this association clear and simple from the beginning gives learners more confidence to start speaking the language.

This book selects the six most commonly used and useful tenses for beginning learners.

Example Sentences

Each of the 101 conjugation pages contains three sample sentences. (All three sentences are also spoken in the corresponding video.) These sentences, loosely inspired by the illustration on the page, show the art of conjugation in practice. The verb form in each sentence is colo(u)r-coded to help match it up to the tables and to help you understand the correct selection of tense and subject on the grid.

Verb Indexes

The 101 verb conjugations in this book are ordered alphabetically by English infinitive. The English Verb Index contains these 101 featured verbs (which appear in blue) as well as related phrasal verbs (with explanations of their meanings). An additional fifty common irregular English verbs are also listed with their principal parts, allowing the deduction of the required verb form.

Independent Learning

101 English Verbs can be used for self-study, or it can be used as a supplement to a teacher-led course. The accompanying videos provide pronunciation (spoken by a native speaker) of the present tense conjugation. Pronunciation of the other conjugations is available online at **www.learnverbs.com**.

Master the Verbs

Once you are confident with each tense, congratulate yourself because you have learned more than 3,600 verb forms—an achievement that can otherwise take a long time to master!

Verb Conjugation in English

Conjugation requires the ability to select the correct verb form. Using this book, this skill is as simple as locating a square on a grid. Simply follow these steps:

- Select the correct verb (use the Verb Index at the back of the book to find the page of the correct model).
- Select the correct person (see the list of personal pronouns in the next section to help you choose the correct row).
- Select the correct tense (see the explanations on pages viii–xv to guide you to choose the correct column).

Select the correct tense ↓

Sub.	Present Simple / Present Cont.	Past Continuous	Past Simple	Future	Conditional	Present Perfect
I	dance – am dancing	was dancing	danced	will dance	would dance	have danced
You	dance – are dancing	were dancing	danced	will dance	would dance	have danced
He She It	dances – is dancing	was dancing	danced	will dance	would dance	has danced
We	dance – are dancing	were dancing	danced	will dance	would dance	have danced
You (pl)	dance – are dancing	were dancing	danced	will dance	would dance	have danced
They	dance – are dancing	were dancing	danced	will dance	would dance	have danced

Select the correct person →

. . . to locate the correct verb form!

The Person of the Verb

To select the correct person, you must know the subject of the verb: who is doing the action. In each conjugation panel, there are six rows. Each row corresponds to a *person*, represented in the first column by the following personal pronouns.

Personal Pronouns

I	the speaker
You	singular: formal and informal
He **She** **It**	male person female person neuter thing
We	plural: includes the speaker
You (pl)	plural: formal and informal
They	plural: any gender

Note the following:

- Pronouns can be grouped by person:

  first person: *I*, *we* (includes the speaker or writer)
  second person: *you* (the person or persons being addressed)
  third person: *he*, *she*, *it*, *they* (the person or persons talked about). The third person is also used for nouns or names of people or animals that are subjects of the sentence.

- Pronouns can also be grouped by number:

  singular: *I*, *you*, *he*, *she*, *it* (one single person, animal, or object)
  plural: *we*, *you*, *they* (more than one person, animal, or object)

- The only subject pronouns that indicate gender are those for third person singular: *he* (masculine), *she* (feminine), and *it* (neuter, no gender).

Verb Tenses

As well as knowing the appropriate verb name (the keyword or infinitive) and the correct person, you also need to select the correct tense. Tenses relate to time: when the action or state takes place. And while there are three basic time states (past, present, and future), there are at least fourteen different tenses in English! But don't worry—many are not frequently used, and this book has selected only six of the most common tenses that you will need. All six tenses are colo(u)r-coded, to help you recognize and learn them. The following pages explain each tense and when it is used. They also indicate how each tense is formed.

Present Simple

Also known as: Present

The present simple tense of regular verbs consists of the basic verb form (the infinitive without the word **to**) in all persons, except for the third person singular. This form (he, she, it) adds **-s** (or **-es** if the verb ends in **-ch, -s, -sh, -x**, and **-z**; **-ses** if the verb ends in **-s**; while a final **-y** is replaced with **-ies**).

Present Simple	I	cook	-
	You	cook	-
	He/She/It	cook	s
	We	cook	-
	You	cook	-
	They	cook	-

The present simple tense is used in English in the following situations:

- for habitual actions that happen regularly (but are not necessarily happening now):

  Cyberdog brings me the newspaper in the morning.

- for descriptions of ongoing states and permanent characteristics:

  I am what I am—a robot with many faults.

- for the subordinate clause of a present/future conditional sentence:

  If you organize your things, you'll find them more easily.

Note the following forms:

- for questions and intensives, use **do** (**does** for third person singular) plus the basic verb form:

Do you like to swim in the sea? When do you swim in the pool?

I do like the pool.

- for negatives, use do not/don't (**does not/doesn't** for third person singular) plus the basic verb form:

I don't like the sea.   **And he doesn't like the pool.**

Present Continuous

Also known as: Present progressive

The present continuous tense of regular verbs is formed with the present simple tense of **to be** plus the present participle. The present participle is formed by adding -*ing* to the basic verb form (removing any final -*e*).

Present Continuous	I	am	cook	ing
	You	are	cook	ing
	He/She/It	is	cook	ing
	We	are	cook	ing
	You	are	cook	ing
	They	are	cook	ing

Forms of the present continuous are commonly contracted: I'm cooking (I am cooking); you're cooking (you are cooking); and similarly with he's/she's/it's/we're/they're cooking.

The present continuous tense is used for actions going on at the current time:

Cyberdog is growing bigger every day.

The different use of the present simple (for habitual actions) and the present continuous (for current actions) is illustrated in this example:

I normally drink coffee in the morning, but today I am drinking fruit juice.

Note the following forms:

- for questions, invert the subject pronoun and the **to be** part of the verb:

Are you swimming in the sea? Why are you swimming in the sea?

- for intensives, add stress to the **to be** part of the verb; for negatives, insert *not* before the present participle:

I *am* swimming in the sea! I'm *not* swimming in the pool.

Past Continuous

Also known as: Past progressive

The past continuous is formed by adding the past simple form of **to be** (*was/ were*) plus the present participle. The present participle is formed by adding *-ing* to the basic verb form (removing any final *-e*).

Past Continuous	I	was	cook	ing
	You	were	cook	ing
	He/She/It	was	cook	ing
	We	were	cook	ing
	You	were	cook	ing
	They	were	cook	ing

The past continuous tense is used in English in the following situations:

- for describing actions that proceeded in the past:

   The Beebots were playing cards all last night.

- for describing actions that were ongoing when something else happened:

   Verbito was swimming in the sea when a school of dolphins swam up.

- for describing background actions such as time and weather:

   It was raining as Verbito and Verbita sat on the beach.

For habitual or repeated actions in the past, use the auxiliary *used to* or *would* plus the base verb form:

   I *used to* swim in the sea.

   Last summer I *would* swim all day in the sea.

Note the following forms:

- for questions, invert the subject pronoun and the **to be** part of the verb:

   Were you swimming in the sea?

- for intensives, add stress to the **to be** part of the verb; for negatives, insert *not* before the present participle:

   I *was* swimming in the sea! I *was* *not* swimming in the pool.

Past Simple

Also known as: Past

The past simple tense of regular verbs is formed by adding **-ed** to the base form of the verb. (Verbs ending in **-e** just add **-d**; verbs ending in **-y** replace it with **-ied**.) See the Verb Index for common irregular past simple verb forms. The form is the same for all persons (except **to be**: **was/were**).

Past Simple	I	cook	ed
	You	cook	ed
	He/She/It	cook	ed
	We	cook	ed
	You	cook	ed
	They	cook	ed

The past simple tense is used in English in the following situations:

- for single actions that happened in the past:

  Verbito **put** all his money on the table.

- for completed actions in the past that were part of a sequence:

  He **entered** through the window, **stole** some valuables, and then **left**.

- for describing an action that occured while another action (in the imperfect) was taking place:

  Verbito **was swimming** in the sea when a school of dolphins **swam** up.

Note the following forms:

- for questions and intensives, use **did** (past simple of **to do**) plus basic verb form:

  Did you **like** to swim in the sea last summer? When **did** you **swim** in the pool?

  I **did like** the pool.

- for negatives, use **did not** (contracted to **didn't**) plus basic verb form:

  I **didn't like** the sea.

Future

Also known as: Simple future

The future is formed from the future form of **to be** (*will*, or its contraction *'ll*) and the base verb form. It is the same for all persons, and there are no irregularities.

Future	I	will	cook
	You	will	cook
	He/She/It	will	cook
	We	will	cook
	You	will	cook
	They	will	cook

The future is used in English in the following situations:

- for describing actions that will happen at some future time:

  Tomorrow I will write some e-mails.

- for describing immediately intended actions or imminent events:

  And now I will show you my invention!

- for describing the consequences of a present/future conditional sentence:

  If you sign here, sir, you will receive this letter.

- for expressing an order (instead of using a command):

  Students, will you please study for the exams!

Note: the verb **to be going** plus the infinitive is used to express future intention:

  Now I'm going to take you for a flight in the time machine.

Note the following forms:

- for questions, invert the subject pronoun and the **to be** part of the verb:

  Will you swim in the sea?

- for intensives, add stress to the **to be** part of the verb; for negatives, insert *not* before the base verb form (*will not* can contract to *won't*):

  I will swim in the sea! I will not swim in the pool.

  If Cyberdog behaves, he will receive a treat.

Conditional

Also described as a modal auxiliary *would*.

The conditional is formed from *would* and the base verb form.

Conditional	I	would	cook
	You	would	cook
	He/She/It	would	cook
	We	would	cook
	You	would	cook
	They	would	cook

The conditional is used in English in the following situations:

- for describing conditional situations that might have happened (but did not):

  If I had a box of matches, I would light this fire easily.

- for asking a question about a hypothetical or possible scenario:

  Would you scream in her situation?

- for softening a demand or wish:

  Would you read aloud that dish, please? I can't pronounce it.

Note the following forms:

- for questions, invert the subject pronoun and the **to be** part of the verb:

  Would you swim in the sea, if you saw sharks?

- for intensives, add stress to the *would* part of the verb; for negatives, insert *not* before the base verb form (*would not* can contract to *wouldn't*):

  I *would* swim in the sea! I would *not* swim in the pool.

Present Perfect

Also known as: Perfect or present perfective

The present perfect tense is formed by combining the present simple form of **to have** plus the past participle. The past participle of regular verbs is formed by adding **-ed** to the basic verb form (add just **-d** to verbs ending in **-e**).

Present Perfect				
	I	have	cook	ed
	You	have	cook	ed
	He/She/It	has	cook	ed
	We	have	cook	ed
	You	have	cook	ed
	They	have	cook	ed

The present perfect tense is used in English for past actions that relate to the present:

> **How many Beebots have you counted so far?**

(The counting is not over yet.)

> **We have forbidden you from jumping.**

(And you are still forbidden from jumping.)

Note the following forms:

- for questions, invert the subject pronoun and the **to be** part of the verb:

> **Have you swum in the sea yet?**

- for intensives, add stress to the **to have** part of the verb; for negatives, insert **not** before the present participle (**have not** can contract to **haven't**):

> **I *have* swum in the sea! But I have n't swum in the pool.**

Command

Also known as: Imperative

The command form is shown in red type on each conjugation page. It is the same form as the second person present simple tense (without the **you**), so the singular and plural forms are the same. The first person plural command is formed by adding **Let's** (= **Let us**).

> **Let's go to the future, Verbito! But don't go over the top!**

The command is used for telling someone to do something, as an order, request, or demand:

> **Students, read this book! It will help you learn English verbs!**

> **Sit down! Relax! Take the weight off your feet!**

> **Finish the race as fast as you can!**

The negative form of the command (for telling someone *not* to do something) is formed by adding **do not** (contracted to **don't**) to the active command:

> **Don't go down there, Cyberdog! You'll regret it!**

The command can be softened by adding ***please*** or using the conditional:

> **Please repair our vehicle! I don't want to be stuck here forever.**

Another way to make a command is to use the future tense:

> **Students, will you please study for the exams!**

Gerund

Also known as: Verbal noun

The gerund is shown opposite the infinitive on each conjugation page. It is formed by adding **-ing** to the verb stem (removing any final **-e**); it is the present participle used as a noun.

The gerund is used in English to describe the action of the verb (often interchangeable with the infinitive):

> **Polishing is very hard work!**

> **I love dancing; it keeps me fit and healthy.**

Reflexive Verbs

Some English verbs refer back to the subject, like the English verb *to wash oneself* (*I wash myself, you wash yourself,* and so on). These verbs include the reflexive pronoun.

Reflexive Pronouns

oneself	the infinitive
myself	the speaker
yourself	singular: formal or informal
himself herself itself	singular
ourselves	plural group, including the speaker
yourselves	plural: formal or informal
themselves	plural group of people or things

Here are a few examples:

He **was kicking** *himself* for being so stupid.

"Clean up after *yourself*!" she would shout.

I think that we **have found** *ourselves* a pet!

Phrasal Verbs

Phrasal verbs are a common feature of English. They consist of a main verb plus another word or words, usually prepositions. The following conjugated verbs are phrasal verbs:

#39 go down	#81 sit down
#40 go out	#95 wake up

Common prepositions used in phrasal verbs include: *around*, *back*, *by*, *down*, *for*, *in*, *on*, *out*, *over*, *through*, *under*, *up*, and *with*. A phrasal verb is often idiomatic; that is, its meaning cannot be guessed from the combined meanings of each individual word in the phrase.

The Verb Index contains common phrasal verb forms of the 101 verbs contained in this book. Several are illustrated in the following example sentences; their meanings are explained in parentheses.

We need to talk through our disagreement, Verbita! (= *To resolve*)

This situation calls for your help, Verbito! (= *Requires*)

Verbita's face lit up when the fire began to blaze. (= *Brightened with pleasure*)

That's why their plans fell through. (= *Did not take place as intended*)

After all that work, he polished off a whole steak. (= *Ate entirely*)

I will not put up with any more losses. (= *Will not accept*)

I will find out what he likes to eat. (= *Discover*)

Verbito has come up with a great idea. (= *Has thought of*)

The Passive

The passive construction is commonly used in English. In passive sentences, the subject is acted upon; that is, the action happens to the subject.

The passive is formed by the appropriate tense of the verb **to be** plus the **past participle**. The **passive infinitive** is shown in olive text beneath the infinitive in each conjugation. See page 109 for a model conjugation.

These examples show the passive forms of the infinitive and each tense:

I love to be kissed! Please don't stop!

Are the files organized alphabetically?

Meanwhile, Verbita's house was being entered by the thief!

The food was cooked at 300 degrees.

What subject will be learned/learnt at school today?

If I had a box of matches, this fire would be lit easily.

All of Verbito's tools have been lost!

If the agent (who performs the action) is mentioned, it usually follows **by**.

This restaurant is liked by all its visitors.

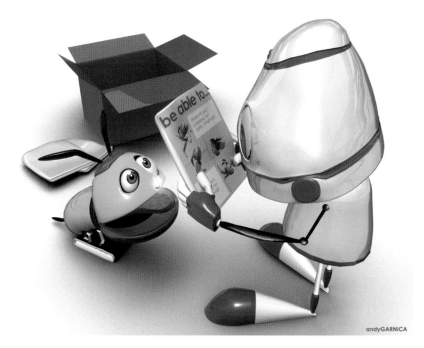

Sub.	Present Simple Present Cont.	Past Continuous	Past Simple	Future	Conditional	Present Perfect
I	am able to (can) – X	was able to	could	will be able to	would be able to (could)	have been able to
You	are able to (can) – X	were able to	could	will be able to	would be able to (could)	have been able to
He She It	is able to (can) – X	was able to	could	will be able to	would be able to (could)	has been able to
We	are able to (can) – X	were able to	could	will be able to	would be able to (could)	have been able to
You (pl)	are able to (can) – X	were able to	could	will be able to	would be able to (could)	have been able to
They	are able to (can) – X	were able to	could	will be able to	would be able to (could)	have been able to

Are you **able to** learn new tricks, Cyberdog?

I **will** not **be able to** go for a walk later.

We **were able to** understand each other.

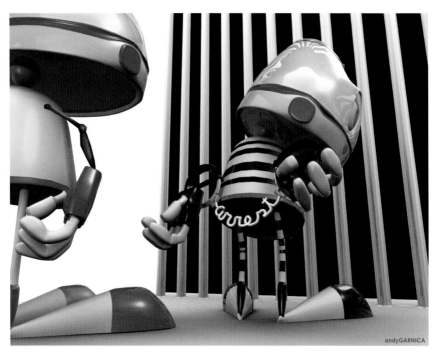

Sub.	Present Simple Present Cont.	Past Continuous	Past Simple	Future	Conditional	Present Perfect
I	arrest – am arresting	was arresting	arrested	will arrest	would arrest	have arrested
You	arrest – are arresting	were arresting	arrested	will arrest	would arrest	have arrested
He She It	arrests – is arresting	was arresting	arrested	will arrest	would arrest	has arrested
We	arrest – are arresting	were arresting	arrested	will arrest	would arrest	have arrested
You (pl)	arrest – are arresting	were arresting	arrested	will arrest	would arrest	have arrested
They	arrest – are arresting	were arresting	arrested	will arrest	would arrest	have arrested

I **arrest** you in the name of the law!

He didn't resist when we **arrested** him.

They **will arrest** all the suspects by tonight.

Sub.	Present Simple Present Cont.	Past Continuous	Past Simple	Future	Conditional	Present Perfect
I	arrive – am arriving	was arriving	arrived	will arrive	would arrive	have arrived
You	arrive – are arriving	were arriving	arrived	will arrive	would arrive	have arrived
He She It	arrives – is arriving	was arriving	arrived	will arrive	would arrive	has arrived
We	arrive – are arriving	were arriving	arrived	will arrive	would arrive	have arrived
You (pl)	arrive – are arriving	were arriving	arrived	will arrive	would arrive	have arrived
They	arrive – are arriving	were arriving	arrived	will arrive	would arrive	have arrived

Verbito is arriving now at gate 4.

I arrived on time as usual.

Verbito and Beebot will arrive together.

3

ask (for)
be asked (for)
ask (for)!

Sub.	Present Simple Present Cont.	Past Continuous	Past Simple	Future	Conditional	Present Perfect
I	ask (for) – am asking (for)	was asking (for)	asked (for)	will ask (for)	would ask (for)	have asked (for)
You	ask (for) – are asking (for)	were asking (for)	asked (for)	will ask (for)	would ask (for)	have asked (for)
He She It	asks (for) – is asking (for)	was asking (for)	asked (for)	will ask (for)	would ask (for)	has asked (for)
We	ask (for) – are asking (for)	were asking (for)	asked (for)	will ask (for)	would ask (for)	have asked (for)
You (pl)	ask (for) – are asking (for)	were asking (for)	asked (for)	will ask (for)	would ask (for)	have asked (for)
They	ask (for) – are asking (for)	were asking (for)	asked (for)	will ask (for)	would ask (for)	have asked (for)

They **ask** for things nicely around here.

We **will ask** for ours when it is our turn.

I have exactly what you **asked** for.

andyGARNICA

Sub.	Present Simple / Present Cont.	Past Continuous	Past Simple	Future	Conditional	Present Perfect
I	am — am being	was being	was	will be	would be	have been
You	are — are being	were being	were	will be	would be	have been
He She It	is — is being	was being	was	will be	would be	has been
We	are — are being	were being	were	will be	would be	have been
You (pl)	are — are being	were being	were	will be	would be	have been
They	are — are being	were being	were	will be	would be	have been

I **am** deep in thought, so keep quiet.

Were you Hamlet in the play, or were you the skull?

Your name **will be** in lights over Broadway.

bring

be brought

bring!

Sub.	Present Simple Present Cont.	Past Continuous	Past Simple	Future	Conditional	Present Perfect
I	bring – am bringing	was bringing	brought	will bring	would bring	have brought
You	bring – are bringing	were bringing	brought	will bring	would bring	have brought
He She It	brings – is bringing	was bringing	brought	will bring	would bring	has brought
We	bring – are bringing	were bringing	brought	will bring	would bring	have brought
You (pl)	bring – are bringing	were bringing	brought	will bring	would bring	have brought
They	bring – are bringing	were bringing	brought	will bring	would bring	have brought

I throw things, and he **brings** them back.

He **brought** back something different.

You **were bringing** back sticks last week.

6

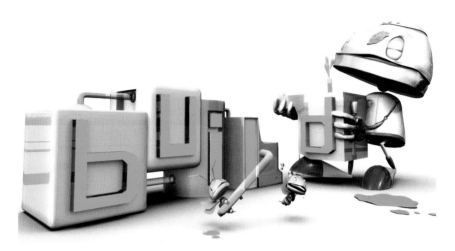

andyGARNICA

Sub.	Present Simple / Present Cont.	Past Continuous	Past Simple	Future	Conditional	Present Perfect
I	build – am building	was building	built	will build	would build	have built
You	build – are building	were building	built	will build	would build	have built
He She It	builds – is building	was building	built	will build	would build	has built
We	build – are building	were building	built	will build	would build	have built
You (pl)	build – are building	were building	built	will build	would build	have built
They	build – are building	were building	built	will build	would build	have built

Show us how you build one like this.

We were building this for an exhibition.

I built it carefully, bit by bit.

7

Sub.	Present Simple Present Cont.	Past Continuous	Past Simple	Future	Conditional	Present Perfect
I	buy – am buying	was buying	bought	will buy	would buy	have bought
You	buy – are buying	were buying	bought	will buy	would buy	have bought
He She It	buys – is buying	was buying	bought	will buy	would buy	has bought
We	buy – are buying	were buying	bought	will buy	would buy	have bought
You (pl)	buy – are buying	were buying	bought	will buy	would buy	have bought
They	buy – are buying	were buying	bought	will buy	would buy	have bought

Verbito and Cyberdog **buy** what food they need every Friday.

I **was buying** what I couldn't afford.

Have you **bought** this as a gift for someone?

andyGARNICA

Sub.	Present Simple Present Cont.	Past Continuous	Past Simple	Future	Conditional	Present Perfect
I	call – am calling	was calling	called	will call	would call	have called
You	call – are calling	were calling	called	will call	would call	have called
He She It	calls – is calling	was calling	called	will call	would call	has called
We	call – are calling	were calling	called	will call	would call	have called
You (pl)	call – are calling	were calling	called	will call	would call	have called
They	call – are calling	were calling	called	will call	would call	have called

I **call** Verbita about three times a day!

Verbita **was calling** me to hear my voice.

We **will call** each other tomorrow morning.

9

andyGARNICA

Sub.	Present Simple Present Cont.	Past Continuous	Past Simple	Future	Conditional	Present Perfect
I	carry – am carrying	was carrying	carried	will carry	would carry	have carried
You	carry – are carrying	were carrying	carried	will carry	would carry	have carried
He She It	carries – is carrying	was carrying	carried	will carry	would carry	has carried
We	carry – are carrying	were carrying	carried	will carry	would carry	have carried
You (pl)	carry – are carrying	were carrying	carried	will carry	would carry	have carried
They	carry – are carrying	were carrying	carried	will carry	would carry	have carried

I am carrying you around today.

We have carried you enough.

Now, you will carry him to the car.

andyGARNICA

Sub.	Present Simple / Present Cont.	Past Continuous	Past Simple	Future	Conditional	Present Perfect
I	change – am changing	was changing	changed	will change	would change	have changed
You	change – are changing	were changing	changed	will change	would change	have changed
He She It	changes – is changing	was changing	changed	will change	would change	has changed
We	change – are changing	were changing	changed	will change	would change	have changed
You (pl)	change – are changing	were changing	changed	will change	would change	have changed
They	change – are changing	were changing	changed	will change	would change	have changed

We **change** their batteries every month.

I think they **have changed** the design.

This process **will change** your life, Beebot!

Sub.	Present Simple Present Cont.	Past Continuous	Past Simple	Future	Conditional	Present Perfect
I	clean – am cleaning	was cleaning	cleaned	will clean	would clean	have cleaned
You	clean – are cleaning	were cleaning	cleaned	will clean	would clean	have cleaned
He She It	cleans – is cleaning	was cleaning	cleaned	will clean	would clean	has cleaned
We	clean – are cleaning	were cleaning	cleaned	will clean	would clean	have cleaned
You (pl)	clean – are cleaning	were cleaning	cleaned	will clean	would clean	have cleaned
They	clean – are cleaning	were cleaning	cleaned	will clean	would clean	have cleaned

You are cleaning together as a team.

They would clean the whole street if you let them.

I have cleaned the windows and doors.

andyGARNICA

Sub.	Present Simple Present Cont.	Past Continuous	Past Simple	Future	Conditional	Present Perfect
I	close – am closing	was closing	closed	will close	would close	have closed
You	close – are closing	were closing	closed	will close	would close	have closed
He She It	closes – is closing	was closing	closed	will close	would close	has closed
We	close – are closing	were closing	closed	will close	would close	have closed
You (pl)	close – are closing	were closing	closed	will close	would close	have closed
They	close – are closing	were closing	closed	will close	would close	have closed

Verbito **closes** the car door on his way home.

I **closed** my car to keep it clean inside.

We heard a thud when you **were closing** it.

Sub.	Present Simple Present Cont.	Past Continuous	Past Simple	Future	Conditional	Present Perfect
I	comb – am combing	was combing	combed	will comb	would comb	have combed
You	comb – are combing	were combing	combed	will comb	would comb	have combed
He She It	combs – is combing	was combing	combed	will comb	would comb	has combed
We	comb – are combing	were combing	combed	will comb	would comb	have combed
You (pl)	comb – are combing	were combing	combed	will comb	would comb	have combed
They	comb – are combing	were combing	combed	will comb	would comb	have combed

I am combing your hair for the party.

I see you have not combed your hair in a while.

We will comb your hair again next week.

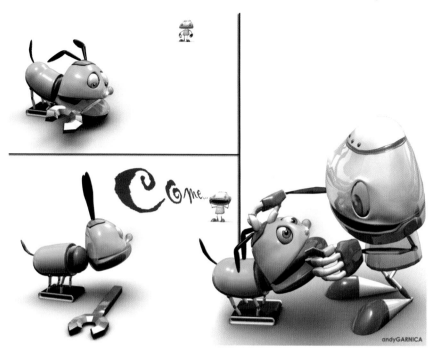

Sub.	Present Simple / Present Cont.	Past Continuous	Past Simple	Future	Conditional	Present Perfect
I	come – am coming	was coming	came	will come	would come	have come
You	come – are coming	were coming	came	will come	would come	have come
He She It	comes – is coming	was coming	came	will come	would come	has come
We	come – are coming	were coming	came	will come	would come	have come
You (pl)	come – are coming	were coming	came	will come	would come	have come
They	come – are coming	were coming	came	will come	would come	have come

Cyberdog **comes** quickly if we call him.

They **came** from another planet.

I will drop everything, and I **will come** running.

cook

be cooked

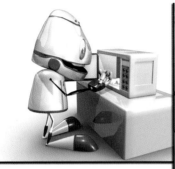

andyGARNICA

Sub.	Present Simple Present Cont.	Past Continuous	Past Simple	Future	Conditional	Present Perfect
I	cook – am cooking	was cooking	cooked	will cook	would cook	have cooked
You	cook – are cooking	were cooking	cooked	will cook	would cook	have cooked
He She It	cooks – is cooking	was cooking	cooked	will cook	would cook	has cooked
We	cook – are cooking	were cooking	cooked	will cook	would cook	have cooked
You (pl)	cook – are cooking	were cooking	cooked	will cook	would cook	have cooked
They	cook – are cooking	were cooking	cooked	will cook	would cook	have cooked

When I **am cooking**, I keep it simple.

You **would cook** for me if you knew how.

We **will cook** a grand meal tomorrow night.

16

Sub.	Present Simple / Present Cont.	Past Continuous	Past Simple	Future	Conditional	Present Perfect
I	count – am counting	was counting	counted	will count	would count	have counted
You	count – are counting	were counting	counted	will count	would count	have counted
He She It	counts – is counting	was counting	counted	will count	would count	has counted
We	count – are counting	were counting	counted	will count	would count	have counted
You (pl)	count – are counting	were counting	counted	will count	would count	have counted
They	count – are counting	were counting	counted	will count	would count	have counted

We **are counting** the Beebots right now.

When you settle down I **will count** you once more.

How many Beebots **have** you **counted** so far?

crash

be crashed

Sub.	Present Simple Present Cont.	Past Continuous	Past Simple	Future	Conditional	Present Perfect
I	crash – am crashing	was crashing	crashed	will crash	would crash	have crashed
You	crash – are crashing	were crashing	crashed	will crash	would crash	have crashed
He She It	crashes – is crashing	was crashing	crashed	will crash	would crash	has crashed
We	crash – are crashing	were crashing	crashed	will crash	would crash	have crashed
You (pl)	crash – are crashing	were crashing	crashed	will crash	would crash	have crashed
They	crash – are crashing	were crashing	crashed	will crash	would crash	have crashed

I **crash** Beebot meetings for fun!

Cyberdog! You **crashed** right through us!

He **will crash** through every party down the hill.

andyGARNICA

Sub.	Present Simple / Present Cont.	Past Continuous	Past Simple	Future	Conditional	Present Perfect
I	create – am creating	was creating	created	will create	would create	have created
You	create – are creating	were creating	created	will create	would create	have created
He She It	creates – is creating	was creating	created	will create	would create	has created
We	create – are creating	were creating	created	will create	would create	have created
You (pl)	create – are creating	were creating	created	will create	would create	have created
They	create – are creating	were creating	created	will create	would create	have created

We **are creating** another Big Bang!

I **will create** a surprise for Verbita.

I wonder if you **have created** a mess.

19

Sub.	Present Simple / Present Cont.	Past Continuous	Past Simple	Future	Conditional	Present Perfect
I	cut – am cutting	was cutting	cut	will cut	would cut	have cut
You	cut – are cutting	were cutting	cut	will cut	would cut	have cut
He She It	cuts – is cutting	was cutting	cut	will cut	would cut	has cut
We	cut – are cutting	were cutting	cut	will cut	would cut	have cut
You (pl)	cut – are cutting	were cutting	cut	will cut	would cut	have cut
They	cut – are cutting	were cutting	cut	will cut	would cut	have cut

I **am cutting** it because it is too long.

First, we **will cut** it into equal parts.

You **would cut** it faster with an electric saw.

Sub.	Present Simple Present Cont.	Past Continuous	Past Simple	Future	Conditional	Present Perfect
I	dance – am dancing	was dancing	danced	will dance	would dance	have danced
You	dance – are dancing	were dancing	danced	will dance	would dance	have danced
He She It	dances – is dancing	was dancing	danced	will dance	would dance	has danced
We	dance – are dancing	were dancing	danced	will dance	would dance	have danced
You (pl)	dance – are dancing	were dancing	danced	will dance	would dance	have danced
They	dance – are dancing	were dancing	danced	will dance	would dance	have danced

We **dance** to keep fit.

I **was dancing** at the party all night.

If only Verbita **would dance** with me!

decide

be decided

andyGARNICA

Sub.	Present Simple / Present Cont.	Past Continuous	Past Simple	Future	Conditional	Present Perfect
I	decide – am deciding	was deciding	decided	will decide	would decide	have decided
You	decide – are deciding	were deciding	decided	will decide	would decide	have decided
He She It	decides – is deciding	was deciding	decided	will decide	would decide	has decided
We	decide – are deciding	were deciding	decided	will decide	would decide	have decided
You (pl)	decide – are deciding	were deciding	decided	will decide	would decide	have decided
They	decide – are deciding	were deciding	decided	will decide	would decide	have decided

You **decide** which one you like better.

Have they **decided** yet?

Make up your mind or I **will decide** for you.

ondyGARNICA

Sub.	Present Simple Present Cont.	Past Continuous	Past Simple	Future	Conditional	Present Perfect
I	direct – am directing	was directing	directed	will direct	would direct	have directed
You	direct – are directing	were directing	directed	will direct	would direct	have directed
He She It	directs – is directing	was directing	directed	will direct	would direct	has directed
We	direct – are directing	were directing	directed	will direct	would direct	have directed
You (pl)	direct – are directing	were directing	directed	will direct	would direct	have directed
They	direct – are directing	were directing	directed	will direct	would direct	have directed

You **direct** operations from there.

Listen to me and I **will direct** you.

He **directed** them through every step.

dream

be dreamed or be dreamt

dreaming

dream!

andyGARNICA

Sub.	Present Simple Present Cont.	Past Continuous	Past Simple	Future	Conditional	Present Perfect
I	dream – am dreaming	was dreaming	dreamed or dreamt	will dream	would dream	have dreamed or have dreamt
You	dream – are dreaming	were dreaming	dreamed or dreamt	will dream	would dream	have dreamed or have dreamt
He She It	dreams – is dreaming	was dreaming	dreamed or dreamt	will dream	would dream	has dreamed or has dreamt
We	dream – are dreaming	were dreaming	dreamed or dreamt	will dream	would dream	have dreamed or have dreamt
You (pl)	dream – are dreaming	were dreaming	dreamed or dreamt	will dream	would dream	have dreamed or have dreamt
They	dream – are dreaming	were dreaming	dreamed or dreamt	will dream	would dream	have dreamed or have dreamt

I **am dreaming**, so please leave me alone.

He **dreamed** he was floating in the sky.

They **have dreamed** every night this week.

24

andyGARNICA

Sub.	Present Simple / Present Cont.	Past Continuous	Past Simple	Future	Conditional	Present Perfect
I	get dressed am getting dressed	was getting dressed	got dressed	will get dressed	would get dressed	have got(ten) dressed
You	get dressed are getting dressed	were getting dressed	got dressed	will get dressed	would get dressed	have got(ten) dressed
He She It	gets dressed is getting dressed	was getting dressed	got dressed	will get dressed	would get dressed	has got(ten) dressed
We	get dressed are getting dressed	were getting dressed	got dressed	will get dressed	would get dressed	have got(ten) dressed
You (pl)	get dressed are getting dressed	were getting dressed	got dressed	will get dressed	would get dressed	have got(ten) dressed
They	get dressed are getting dressed	were getting dressed	got dressed	will get dressed	would get dressed	have got(ten) dressed

You **are getting dressed** in your Sunday best.

He **got dressed** before I brushed his hair.

We **will get dressed** when the guests arrive.

25

drink

be drunk

drink!

Sub.	Present Simple / Present Cont.	Past Continuous	Past Simple	Future	Conditional	Present Perfect
I	drink – am drinking	was drinking	drank	will drink	would drink	have drunk
You	drink – are drinking	were drinking	drank	will drink	would drink	have drunk
He She It	drinks – is drinking	was drinking	drank	will drink	would drink	has drunk
We	drink – are drinking	were drinking	drank	will drink	would drink	have drunk
You (pl)	drink – are drinking	were drinking	drank	will drink	would drink	have drunk
They	drink – are drinking	were drinking	drank	will drink	would drink	have drunk

Verbito **is drinking** like there's no tomorrow.

We **will drink** everything in the refrigerator.

I **have drunk** six of these already.

andyGARNiCA

Sub.	Present Simple Present Cont.	Past Continuous	Past Simple	Future	Conditional	Present Perfect
I	drive – am driving	was driving	drove	will drive	would drive	have driven
You	drive – are driving	were driving	drove	will drive	would drive	have driven
He She It	drives – is driving	was driving	drove	will drive	would drive	has driven
We	drive – are driving	were driving	drove	will drive	would drive	have driven
You (pl)	drive – are driving	were driving	drove	will drive	would drive	have driven
They	drive – are driving	were driving	drove	will drive	would drive	have driven

We **drive** from one planet to the next.

They **were driving** like mad robots.

I **will drive**, and you watch the stars.

Sub.	Present Simple / Present Cont.	Past Continuous	Past Simple	Future	Conditional	Present Perfect
I	eat – am eating	was eating	ate	will eat	would eat	have eaten
You	eat – are eating	were eating	ate	will eat	would eat	have eaten
He She It	eats – is eating	was eating	ate	will eat	would eat	has eaten
We	eat – are eating	were eating	ate	will eat	would eat	have eaten
You (pl)	eat – are eating	were eating	ate	will eat	would eat	have eaten
They	eat – are eating	were eating	ate	will eat	would eat	have eaten

Beebots **eat** whatever you offer them.

I **have eaten** one of these before.

You **ate** the whole cookie yourself.

andyGARNICA

Sub.	Present Simple Present Cont.	Past Continuous	Past Simple	Future	Conditional	Present Perfect
I	enter – am entering	was entering	entered	will enter	would enter	have entered
You	enter – are entering	were entering	entered	will enter	would enter	have entered
He She It	enters – is entering	was entering	entered	will enter	would enter	has entered
We	enter – are entering	were entering	entered	will enter	would enter	have entered
You (pl)	enter – are entering	were entering	entered	will enter	would enter	have entered
They	enter – are entering	were entering	entered	will enter	would enter	have entered

We **enter** as the red lights go green.

I **will enter** first, and then you follow.

They **were entering** one at a time.

fall

falling

fall!

andyGARNICA

Sub.	Present Simple Present Cont.	Past Continuous	Past Simple	Future	Conditional	Present Perfect
I	fall – am falling	was falling	fell	will fall	would fall	have fallen
You	fall – are falling	were falling	fell	will fall	would fall	have fallen
He She It	falls – is falling	was falling	fell	will fall	would fall	has fallen
We	fall – are falling	were falling	fell	will fall	would fall	have fallen
You (pl)	fall – are falling	were falling	fell	will fall	would fall	have fallen
They	fall – are falling	were falling	fell	will fall	would fall	have fallen

He **falls** off his chair at least once a day.

Verbito! You **fell**! Are you OK?

I nearly squashed them as I **was falling**.

andyGARNICA

Sub.	Present Simple / Present Cont.	Past Continuous	Past Simple	Future	Conditional	Present Perfect
I	fight — am fighting	was fighting	fought	will fight	would fight	have fought
You	fight — are fighting	were fighting	fought	will fight	would fight	have fought
He She It	fights — is fighting	was fighting	fought	will fight	would fight	has fought
We	fight — are fighting	were fighting	fought	will fight	would fight	have fought
You (pl)	fight — are fighting	were fighting	fought	will fight	would fight	have fought
They	fight — are fighting	were fighting	fought	will fight	would fight	have fought

Easy! We **are** not **fighting** for real!

I **will fight** with the green sword next time.

They **fought** till their batteries went red.

andyGARNICA

Sub.	Present Simple / Present Cont.	Past Continuous	Past Simple	Future	Conditional	Present Perfect
I	find – am finding	was finding	found	will find	would find	have found
You	find – are finding	were finding	found	will find	would find	have found
He She It	finds – is finding	was finding	found	will find	would find	has found
We	find – are finding	were finding	found	will find	would find	have found
You (pl)	find – are finding	were finding	found	will find	would find	have found
They	find – are finding	were finding	found	will find	would find	have found

We **find** many lost dogs asleep under a tree.

Officer! You **found** Cyberdog!

I am so happy we **have found** him at last.

finish

andyGARNICA

Sub.	Present Simple / Present Cont.	Past Continuous	Past Simple	Future	Conditional	Present Perfect
I	finish / — / am finishing	was finishing	finished	will finish	would finish	have finished
You	finish / — / are finishing	were finishing	finished	will finish	would finish	have finished
He She It	finishes / — / is finishing	was finishing	finished	will finish	would finish	has finished
We	finish / — / are finishing	were finishing	finished	will finish	would finish	have finished
You (pl)	finish / — / are finishing	were finishing	finished	will finish	would finish	have finished
They	finish / — / are finishing	were finishing	finished	will finish	would finish	have finished

I **finish** all my races with a sprint.

They **have finished** in record time.

You **would finish** more quickly if you went faster.

andyGARNICA

Sub.	Present Simple Present Cont.	Past Continuous	Past Simple	Future	Conditional	Present Perfect
I	follow am following	was following	followed	will follow	would follow	have followed
You	follow are following	were following	followed	will follow	would follow	have followed
He She It	follows is following	was following	followed	will follow	would follow	has followed
We	follow are following	were following	followed	will follow	would follow	have followed
You (pl)	follow are following	were following	followed	will follow	would follow	have followed
They	follow are following	were following	followed	will follow	would follow	have followed

I **follow** the cookies only up to a point.

He **followed** the scent for half a mile.

We **will follow** him as he goes for the trap.

34

forbid

andyGARNICA

Sub.	Present Simple Present Cont.	Past Continuous	Past Simple	Future	Conditional	Present Perfect
I	forbid am forbidding	was forbidding	forbade	will forbid	would forbid	have forbidden
You	forbid are forbidding	were forbidding	forbade	will forbid	would forbid	have forbidden
He She It	forbids is forbidding	was forbidding	forbade	will forbid	would forbid	has forbidden
We	forbid are forbidding	were forbidding	forbade	will forbid	would forbid	have forbidden
You (pl)	forbid are forbidding	were forbidding	forbade	will forbid	would forbid	have forbidden
They	forbid are forbidding	were forbidding	forbade	will forbid	would forbid	have forbidden

The sign **forbids** us from entering.

We **have forbidden** you from jumping.

If they asked to enter, I **would forbid** it.

35

Sub.	Present Simple Present Cont.	Past Continuous	Past Simple	Future	Conditional	Present Perfect
I	forget – am forgetting	was forgetting	forgot	will forget	would forget	have forgotten
You	forget – are forgetting	were forgetting	forgot	will forget	would forget	have forgotten
He She It	forgets – is forgetting	was forgetting	forgot	will forget	would forget	has forgotten
We	forget – are forgetting	were forgetting	forgot	will forget	would forget	have forgotten
You (pl)	forget – are forgetting	were forgetting	forgot	will forget	would forget	have forgotten
They	forget – are forgetting	were forgetting	forgot	will forget	would forget	have forgotten

Are you **forgetting** something, dear?

Sorry! I **forgot** the broccoli again.

We **have forgotten** the ice cream!

Sub.	Present Simple Present Cont.	Past Continuous	Past Simple	Future	Conditional	Present Perfect
I	give – am giving	was giving	gave	will give	would give	have given
You	give – are giving	were giving	gave	will give	would give	have given
He She It	gives – is giving	was giving	gave	will give	would give	has given
We	give – are giving	were giving	gave	will give	would give	have given
You (pl)	give – are giving	were giving	gave	will give	would give	have given
They	give – are giving	were giving	gave	will give	would give	have given

I **am giving** you flowers for no reason.

You **gave** me chocolates last week.

He **would give** her flowers every day.

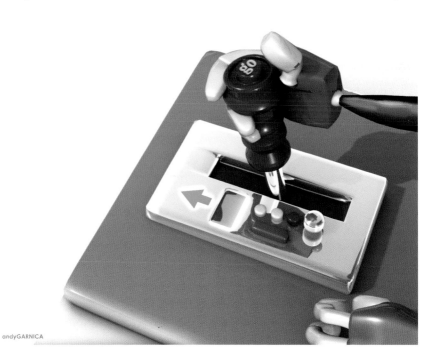

andyGARNICA

Sub.	Present Simple Present Cont.	Past Continuous	Past Simple	Future	Conditional	Present Perfect
I	go – am going	was going	went	will go	would go	have gone
You	go – are going	were going	went	will go	would go	have gone
He She It	goes – is going	was going	went	will go	would go	has gone
We	go – are going	were going	went	will go	would go	have gone
You (pl)	go – are going	were going	went	will go	would go	have gone
They	go – are going	were going	went	will go	would go	have gone

You press here and you just **go**!

She **was going** as fast as possible.

We **have been going** very quickly.

go down

Sub.	Present Simple Present Cont.	Past Continuous	Past Simple	Future	Conditional	Present Perfect
I	go down – am going down	was going down	went down	will go down	would go down	have gone down
You	go down – are going down	were going down	went down	will go down	would go down	have gone down
He She It	goes down – is going down	was going down	went down	will go down	would go down	has gone down
We	go down – are going down	were going down	went down	will go down	would go down	have gone down
You (pl)	go down – are going down	were going down	went down	will go down	would go down	have gone down
They	go down – are going down	were going down	went down	will go down	would go down	have gone down

They **are going down** to the parking lot.

We had a chat as we **went down**.

She **was going down** in the elevator.

go out
be gone out

andyGARNICA

Sub.	Present Simple Present Cont.	Past Continuous	Past Simple	Future	Conditional	Present Perfect
I	go out – am going out	was going out	went out	will go out	would go out	have gone out
You	go out – are going out	were going out	went out	will go out	would go out	have gone out
He She It	goes out – is going out	was going out	went out	will go out	would go out	has gone out
We	go out – are going out	were going out	went out	will go out	would go out	have gone out
You (pl)	go out – are going out	were going out	went out	will go out	would go out	have gone out
They	go out – are going out	were going out	went out	will go out	would go out	have gone out

I **am going out** through a hole in the ceiling.

He **went out** as soon as he could.

You **would go out** every day if we let you.

andyGARNICA

Sub.	Present Simple Present Cont.	Past Continuous	Past Simple	Future	Conditional	Present Perfect
I	grow – am growing	was growing	grew	will grow	would grow	have grown
You	grow – are growing	were growing	grew	will grow	would grow	have grown
He She It	grows – is growing	was growing	grew	will grow	would grow	has grown
We	grow – are growing	were growing	grew	will grow	would grow	have grown
You (pl)	grow – are growing	were growing	grew	will grow	would grow	have grown
They	grow – are growing	were growing	grew	will grow	would grow	have grown

He **grows** almost instantly with this stuff.

She blinked and I **grew** by two feet.

How you **have grown**, Verbito!

41

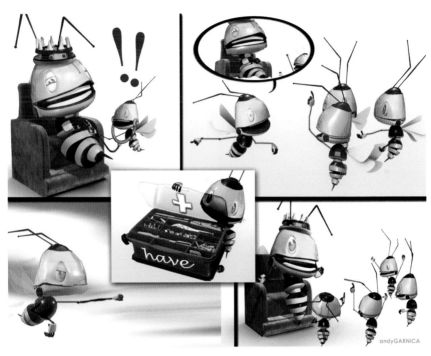

Sub.	Present Simple / Present Cont.	Past Continuous	Past Simple	Future	Conditional	Present Perfect
I	have – am having	was having	had	will have	would have	have had
You	have – are having	were having	had	will have	would have	have had
He She It	has – is having	was having	had	will have	would have	has had
We	have – are having	were having	had	will have	would have	have had
You (pl)	have – are having	were having	had	will have	would have	have had
They	have – are having	were having	had	will have	would have	have had

I **have** this bug in my royal stomach!

She **has had** a ferocious stomachache.

We **will have** her medication ready soon.

andyGARNICA

Sub.	Present Simple Present Cont.	Past Continuous	Past Simple	Future	Conditional	Present Perfect
I	hear – am hearing	was hearing	heard	will hear	would hear	have heard
You	hear – are hearing	were hearing	heard	will hear	would hear	have heard
He She It	hears – is hearing	was hearing	heard	will hear	would hear	has heard
We	hear – are hearing	were hearing	heard	will hear	would hear	have heard
You (pl)	hear – are hearing	were hearing	heard	will hear	would hear	have heard
They	hear – are hearing	were hearing	heard	will hear	would hear	have heard

We **hear** those Beebots nearly every night of the week.

You **would hear** it even more loudly if you stood over there.

I **heard** a lot of noise coming from the Beebot party.

Sub.	Present Simple / Present Cont.	Past Continuous	Past Simple	Future	Conditional	Present Perfect
I	jump – am jumping	was jumping	jumped	will jump	would jump	have jumped
You	jump – are jumping	were jumping	jumped	will jump	would jump	have jumped
He She It	jumps – is jumping	was jumping	jumped	will jump	would jump	has jumped
We	jump – are jumping	were jumping	jumped	will jump	would jump	have jumped
You (pl)	jump – are jumping	were jumping	jumped	will jump	would jump	have jumped
They	jump – are jumping	were jumping	jumped	will jump	would jump	have jumped

They **are jumping** and having fun.

He **jumped** onto the trampoline first.

Verbita **was jumping** higher each time.

Sub.	Present Simple Present Cont.	Past Continuous	Past Simple	Future	Conditional	Present Perfect
I	kick – am kicking	was kicking	kicked	will kick	would kick	have kicked
You	kick – are kicking	were kicking	kicked	will kick	would kick	have kicked
He She It	kicks – is kicking	was kicking	kicked	will kick	would kick	has kicked
We	kick – are kicking	were kicking	kicked	will kick	would kick	have kicked
You (pl)	kick – are kicking	were kicking	kicked	will kick	would kick	have kicked
They	kick – are kicking	were kicking	kicked	will kick	would kick	have kicked

Verbito **kicks** the ball with all his might.

I **would kick** it farther, but my knee hurts.

We **were kicking** the ball around the park.

kiss

be kissed

andyGARNICA

Sub.	Present Simple Present Cont.	Past Continuous	Past Simple	Future	Conditional	Present Perfect
I	kiss – am kissing	was kissing	kissed	will kiss	would kiss	have kissed
You	kiss – are kissing	were kissing	kissed	will kiss	would kiss	have kissed
He She It	kisses – is kissing	was kissing	kissed	will kiss	would kiss	has kissed
We	kiss – are kissing	were kissing	kissed	will kiss	would kiss	have kissed
You (pl)	kiss – are kissing	were kissing	kissed	will kiss	would kiss	have kissed
They	kiss – are kissing	were kissing	kissed	will kiss	would kiss	have kissed

You **kiss** like those girls in the movies.

Verbita **kissed** me, and I almost fainted.

I **would kiss** you even if you were a frog.

Sub.	Present Simple Present Cont.	Past Continuous	Past Simple	Future	Conditional	Present Perfect
I	know – x	was knowing	knew	will know	would know	have known
You	know – x	were knowing	knew	will know	would know	have known
He She It	knows – x	was knowing	knew	will know	would know	has known
We	know – x	were knowing	knew	will know	would know	have known
You (pl)	know – x	were knowing	knew	will know	would know	have known
They	know – x	were knowing	knew	will know	would know	have known

You both **know** the rules of the game.

We **will know** the winner very soon.

If she **knew**, she would answer before him.

47

andyGARNICA

Sub.	Present Simple / Present Cont.	Past Continuous	Past Simple	Future	Conditional	Present Perfect
I	learn – am learning	was learning	learned or learnt	will learn	would learn	have learned or have learnt
You	learn – are learning	were learning	learned or learnt	will learn	would learn	have learned or have learnt
He She It	learns – is learning	was learning	learned or learnt	will learn	would learn	has learned or has learnt
We	learn – are learning	were learning	learned or learnt	will learn	would learn	have learned or have learnt
You (pl)	learn – are learning	were learning	learned or learnt	will learn	would learn	have learned or have learnt
They	learn – are learning	were learning	learned or learnt	will learn	would learn	have learned or have learnt

Beebots **learn** something new each day.

Yesterday I **learned** how to make honey.

If we were mosquitoes, we **would learn** about blood.

48

Sub.	Present Simple / Present Cont.	Past Continuous	Past Simple	Future	Conditional	Present Perfect
I	lie – am lying	was lying	lied	will lie	would lie	have lied
You	lie – are lying	were lying	lied	will lie	would lie	have lied
He She It	lies – is lying	was lying	lied	will lie	would lie	has lied
We	lie – are lying	were lying	lied	will lie	would lie	have lied
You (pl)	lie – are lying	were lying	lied	will lie	would lie	have lied
They	lie – are lying	were lying	lied	will lie	would lie	have lied

You **are lying** about those flowers.

She **would lie**, too, but only if they were white lies.

I **lied**, and then I felt terrible afterward.

andyGARNICA

Sub.	Present Simple / Present Cont.	Past Continuous	Past Simple	Future	Conditional	Present Perfect
I	light – am lighting	was lighting	lit	will light	would light	have lit
You	light – are lighting	were lighting	lit	will light	would light	have lit
He She It	lights – is lighting	was lighting	lit	will light	would light	has lit
We	light – are lighting	were lighting	lit	will light	would light	have lit
You (pl)	light – are lighting	were lighting	lit	will light	would light	have lit
They	light – are lighting	were lighting	lit	will light	would light	have lit

I **am lighting** up the whole area.

Both my fingers **have lit** up the bulb.

He **would light** a tree if it were Christmas.

Sub.	Present Simple / Present Cont.	Past Continuous	Past Simple	Future	Conditional	Present Perfect
I	like – am liking	was liking	liked	will like	would like	have liked
You	like – are liking	were liking	liked	will like	would like	have liked
He She It	likes – is liking	was liking	liked	will like	would like	has liked
We	like – are liking	were liking	liked	will like	would like	have liked
You (pl)	like – are liking	were liking	liked	will like	would like	have liked
They	like – are liking	were liking	liked	will like	would like	have liked

Cyberdog **likes** these cookies so much he will do anything to get one.

You **would like** another cookie, wouldn't you?

I **liked** being a Cyberdog because of the treats.

Sub.	Present Simple / Present Cont.	Past Continuous	Past Simple	Future	Conditional	Present Perfect
I	live — am living	was living	lived	will live	would live	have lived
You	live — are living	were living	lived	will live	would live	have lived
He She It	lives — is living	was living	lived	will live	would live	has lived
We	live — are living	were living	lived	will live	would live	have lived
You (pl)	live — are living	were living	lived	will live	would live	have lived
They	live — are living	were living	lived	will live	would live	have lived

We **live** in a place that's quite green.

If you **were living** in that house, you would be my neighbor.

They **have lived** here all their lives.

lose!

be lost

andyGARNICA

Sub.	Present Simple / Present Cont.	Past Continuous	Past Simple	Future	Conditional	Present Perfect
I	lose – am losing	was losing	lost	will lose	would lose	have lost
You	lose – are losing	were losing	lost	will lose	would lose	have lost
He She It	loses – is losing	was losing	lost	will lose	would lose	has lost
We	lose – are losing	were losing	lost	will lose	would lose	have lost
You (pl)	lose – are losing	were losing	lost	will lose	would lose	have lost
They	lose – arc losing	were losing	lost	will lose	would lose	have lost

It is not easy when she **loses** her pet.

I **lost** count of the posters we put up.

We **will** never **lose** hope of finding him.

love

be loved

love!

andyGARNICA

Sub.	Present Simple / Present Cont.	Past Continuous	Past Simple	Future	Conditional	Present Perfect
I	love — am loving	was loving	loved	will love	would love	have loved
You	love — are loving	were loving	loved	will love	would love	have loved
He She It	loves — is loving	was loving	loved	will love	would love	has loved
We	love — are loving	were loving	loved	will love	would love	have loved
You (pl)	love — are loving	were loving	loved	will love	would love	have loved
They	love — are loving	were loving	loved	will love	would love	have loved

They **love** every moment together.

We **will love** each other forever.

You **have loved** one another from day one.

make

Sub.	Present Simple / Present Cont.	Past Continuous	Past Simple	Future	Conditional	Present Perfect
I	make – am making	was making	made	will make	would make	have made
You	make – are making	were making	made	will make	would make	have made
He She It	makes – is making	was making	made	will make	would make	has made
We	make – are making	were making	made	will make	would make	have made
You (pl)	make – are making	were making	made	will make	would make	have made
They	make – are making	were making	made	will make	would make	have made

I **am making** things with my hands.

Here is something we **made** earlier.

We **will make** a few more next week.

get married

be got(ten) married

Sub.	Present Simple Present Cont.	Past Continuous	Past Simple	Future	Conditional	Present Perfect
I	get married am getting married	was getting married	got married	will get married	would get married	have got(ten) married
You	get married are getting married	were getting married	got married	will get married	would get married	have got(ten) married
He She It	gets married is getting married	was getting married	got married	will get married	would get married	has got(ten) married
We	get married are getting married	were getting married	got married	will get married	would get married	have got(ten) married
You (pl)	get married are getting married	were getting married	got married	will get married	would get married	have got(ten) married
They	get married are getting married	were getting married	got married	will get married	would get married	have got(ten) married

Verbito and Verbita are getting married.

You will get married by pressing here.

Cyberdog was there when I got married.

andyGARNICA

Sub.	Present Simple Present Cont.	Past Continuous	Past Simple	Future	Conditional	Present Perfect
I	open – am opening	was opening	opened	will open	would open	have opened
You	open – are opening	were opening	opened	will open	would open	have opened
He She It	opens – is opening	was opening	opened	will open	would open	has opened
We	open – are opening	were opening	opened	will open	would open	have opened
You (pl)	open – are opening	were opening	opened	will open	would open	have opened
They	open – are opening	were opening	opened	will open	would open	have opened

Verbito opens his drink with a flick of his finger.

I would open one for you, but this is my last one.

You opened it and released the bubbles.

57

Sub.	Present Simple Present Cont.	Past Continuous	Past Simple	Future	Conditional	Present Perfect
I	organize – am organizing	was organizing	organized	will organize	would organize	have organized
You	organize – are organizing	were organizing	organized	will organize	would organize	have organized
He She It	organizes – is organizing	was organizing	organized	will organize	would organize	has organized
We	organize – are organizing	were organizing	organized	will organize	would organize	have organized
You (pl)	organize – are organizing	were organizing	organized	will organize	would organize	have organized
They	organize – are organizing	were organizing	organized	will organize	would organize	have organized

We **organize** our files as neatly as possible.

I **organized** everything by date and number.

They were impressed by how you **have organized** your documents.

andyGARNICA

Sub.	Present Simple / Present Cont.	Past Continuous	Past Simple	Future	Conditional	Present Perfect
I	paint – am painting	was painting	painted	will paint	would paint	have painted
You	paint – are painting	were painting	painted	will paint	would paint	have painted
He She It	paints – is painting	was painting	painted	will paint	would paint	has painted
We	paint – are painting	were painting	painted	will paint	would paint	have painted
You (pl)	paint – are painting	were painting	painted	will paint	would paint	have painted
They	paint – are painting	were painting	painted	will paint	would paint	have painted

Verbito gets messy when he paints .

You have painted a masterpiece.

I will paint a picture of Verbita.

Sub.	Present Simple Present Cont.	Past Continuous	Past Simple	Future	Conditional	Present Perfect
I	pay – am paying	was paying	paid	will pay	would pay	have paid
You	pay – are paying	were paying	paid	will pay	would pay	have paid
He She It	pays – is paying	was paying	paid	will pay	would pay	has paid
We	pay – are paying	were paying	paid	will pay	would pay	have paid
You (pl)	pay – are paying	were paying	paid	will pay	would pay	have paid
They	pay – are paying	were paying	paid	will pay	would pay	have paid

I **am paying** for everything by credit card.

He **would pay** in cash but he doesn't have enough.

They **paid** before leaving the store.

Sub.	Present Simple Present Cont.	Past Continuous	Past Simple	Future	Conditional	Present Perfect
I	play – am playing	was playing	played	will play	would play	have played
You	play – are playing	were playing	played	will play	would play	have played
He She It	plays is playing	was playing	played	will play	would play	has played
We	play – are playing	were playing	played	will play	would play	have played
You (pl)	play – are playing	were playing	played	will play	would play	have played
They	play – are playing	were playing	played	will play	would play	have played

He **plays** games all day, every day.

You **played** this same game about ten times already.

They **were playing** these games until their thumbs fell off.

61

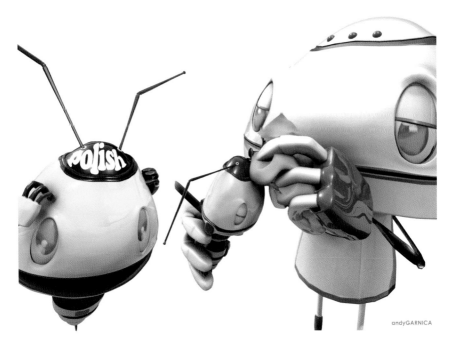

Sub.	Present Simple Present Cont.	Past Continuous	Past Simple	Future	Conditional	Present Perfect
I	polish – am polishing	was polishing	polished	will polish	would polish	have polished
You	polish – are polishing	were polishing	polished	will polish	would polish	have polished
He She It	polishes is polishing	was polishing	polished	will polish	would polish	has polished
We	polish – are polishing	were polishing	polished	will polish	would polish	have polished
You (pl)	polish – are polishing	were polishing	polished	will polish	would polish	have polished
They	polish – are polishing	were polishing	polished	will polish	would polish	have polished

We **polish** their heads to make them shiny.

You **will polish** a couple of Beebots before they set off.

I **have polished** them, and they are now ready to go.

andyGARNICA

Sub.	Present Simple Present Cont.	Past Continuous	Past Simple	Future	Conditional	Present Perfect
I	put – am putting	was putting	put	will put	would put	have put
You	put – are putting	were putting	put	will put	would put	have put
He She It	puts – is putting	was putting	put	will put	would put	has put
We	put – are putting	were putting	put	will put	would put	have put
You (pl)	put – are putting	were putting	put	will put	would put	have put
They	put – are putting	were putting	put	will put	would put	have put

He **puts** some away for a rainy day.

You **have put** a lot of change in there.

I **put** a small fortune in this jar.

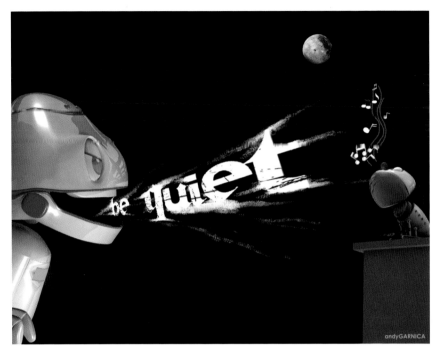

Sub.	Present Simple Present Cont.	Past Continuous	Past Simple	Future	Conditional	Present Perfect
I	am quiet – am being quiet	was being quiet	was quiet	will be quiet	would be quiet	have been quiet
You	are quiet – are being quiet	were being quiet	were quiet	will be quiet	would be quiet	have been quiet
He She It	is quiet – is being quiet	was being quiet	was quiet	will be quiet	would be quiet	has been quiet
We	are quiet – are being quiet	were being quiet	were quiet	will be quiet	would be quiet	have been quiet
You (pl)	are quiet – are being quiet	were being quiet	were quiet	will be quiet	would be quiet	have been quiet
They	are quiet – are being quiet	were being quiet	were quiet	will be quiet	would be quiet	have been quiet

Usually, he **is quiet** around this time.

I **have been quiet** on most nights.

Everyone **will be quiet** again at sunrise.

andyGARNICA

Sub.	Present Simple / Present Cont.	Past Continuous	Past Simple	Future	Conditional	Present Perfect
I	quit – am quitting	was quitting	quitted	will quit	would quit	have quitted/ quit
You	quit – are quitting	were quitting	quitted	will quit	would quit	have quitted/ quit
He She It	quits – is quitting	was quitting	quitted	will quit	would quit	has quitted/ quit
We	quit – are quitting	were quitting	quitted	will quit	would quit	have quitted/ quit
You (pl)	quit – are quitting	were quitting	quitted	will quit	would quit	have quitted/ quit
They	quit – are quitting	were quitting	quitted	will quit	would quit	have quitted/ quit

My machine **is quitting** too often.

I **will quit** and go home soon.

He **would quit** now if he had the choice.

rain

be rained

rain!

andyGARNICA

Sub.	Present Simple Present Cont.	Past Continuous	Past Simple	Future	Conditional	Present Perfect
It	rains – is raining	was raining	rained	will rain	would rain	has rained

It **is raining** heavily today, Cyberdog!

Do you think it **will rain** tomorrow too?

It **rained** every time we went for a walk.

andyGARNICA

Sub.	Present Simple / Present Cont.	Past Continuous	Past Simple	Future	Conditional	Present Perfect
I	read – am reading	was reading	read	will read	would read	have read
You	read – are reading	were reading	read	will read	would read	have read
He She It	reads – is reading	was reading	read	will read	would read	has read
We	read – are reading	were reading	read	will read	would read	have read
You (pl)	read – are reading	were reading	read	will read	would read	have read
They	read – are reading	were reading	read	will read	would read	have read

We **read** big, fat books together.

I **will read** this page, and you read the next.

They **have read** this book over and over again.

andyGARNICA

Sub.	Present Simple Present Cont.	Past Continuous	Past Simple	Future	Conditional	Present Perfect
I	receive – am receiving	was receiving	received	will receive	would receive	have received
You	receive – are receiving	were receiving	received	will receive	would receive	have received
He She It	receives – is receiving	was receiving	received	will receive	would receive	has received
We	receive – are receiving	were receiving	received	will receive	would receive	have received
You (pl)	receive – are receiving	were receiving	received	will receive	would receive	have received
They	receive – are receiving	were receiving	received	will receive	would receive	have received

We **receive** gifts on special occasions.

Verbita **received** a big surprise today.

I **have received** some wonderful gifts.

record

06/03/2982   ● record

andyGARNICA

Sub.	Present Simple / Present Cont.	Past Continuous	Past Simple	Future	Conditional	Present Perfect
I	record – am recording	was recording	recorded	will record	would record	have recorded
You	record – are recording	were recording	recorded	will record	would record	have recorded
He She It	records – is recording	was recording	recorded	will record	would record	has recorded
We	record – are recording	were recording	recorded	will record	would record	have recorded
You (pl)	record – are recording	were recording	recorded	will record	would record	have recorded
They	record – are recording	were recording	recorded	will record	would record	have recorded

He plays up when I am recording .

We recorded every move he made.

They would record all Cyberdog's bath times, but he is too shy.

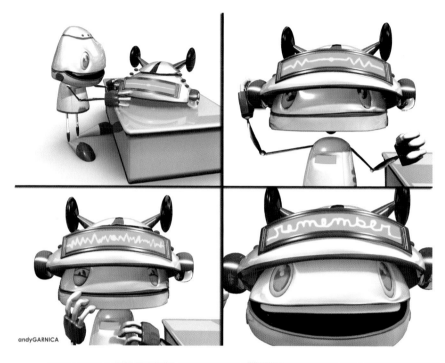

andyGARNICA

Sub.	Present Simple Present Cont.	Past Continuous	Past Simple	Future	Conditional	Present Perfect
I	remember am remembering	was remembering	remembered	will remember	would remember	have remembered
You	remember are remembering	were remembering	remembered	will remember	would remember	have remembered
He She It	remembers is remembering	was remembering	remembered	will remember	would remember	has remembered
We	remember are remembering	were remembering	remembered	will remember	would remember	have remembered
You (pl)	remember are remembering	were remembering	remembered	will remember	would remember	have remembered
They	remember are remembering	were remembering	remembered	will remember	would remember	have remembered

I **remember** the day I received this as a gift from Verbita.

If you wore it all the time, you **would remember** everything.

From now on, he **will remember** every detail.

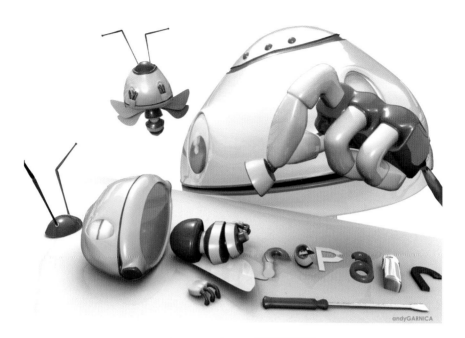

Sub.	Present Simple Present Cont.	Past Continuous	Past Simple	Future	Conditional	Present Perfect
I	repair – am repairing	was repairing	repaired	will repair	would repair	have repaired
You	repair – are repairing	were repairing	repaired	will repair	would repair	have repaired
He She It	repairs – is repairing	was repairing	repaired	will repair	would repair	has repaired
We	repair – are repairing	were repairing	repaired	will repair	would repair	have repaired
You (pl)	repair – are repairing	were repairing	repaired	will repair	would repair	have repaired
They	repair – are repairing	were repairing	repaired	will repair	would repair	have repaired

They **repair** Beebots in this workshop.

I **have repaired** Beebots since I was four.

We **would repair** more if we had the staff.

Sub.	Present Simple Present Cont.	Past Continuous	Past Simple	Future	Conditional	Present Perfect
I	return – am returning	was returning	returned	will return	would return	have returned
You	return – are returning	were returning	returned	will return	would return	have returned
He She It	returns – is returning	was returning	returned	will return	would return	has returned
We	return – are returning	were returning	returned	will return	would return	have returned
You (pl)	return – are returning	were returning	returned	will return	would return	have returned
They	return – are returning	were returning	returned	will return	would return	have returned

I **am returning** home to face the music.

He **returned** home to a wonderful surprise.

You **have returned** late because your spaceship was delayed.

run! be run

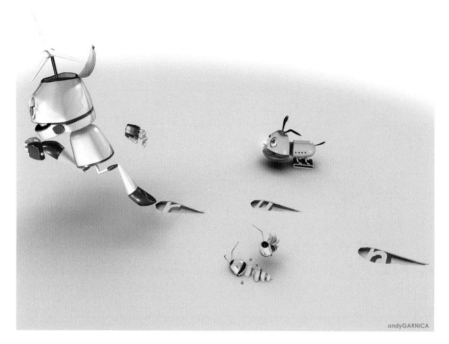

Sub.	Present Simple Present Cont.	Past Continuous	Past Simple	Future	Conditional	Present Perfect
I	run – am running	was running	ran	will run	would run	have run
You	run – are running	were running	ran	will run	would run	have run
He She It	runs – is running	was running	ran	will run	would run	has run
We	run – are running	were running	ran	will run	would run	have run
You (pl)	run – are running	were running	ran	will run	would run	have run
They	run – are running	were running	ran	will run	would run	have run

Verbito **runs** easily because of the weak gravity up there.

I nearly stepped on a Beebot as I **ran**.

We **would run** to Mars and back, but these are the wrong shoes for running.

andyGARNICA

Sub.	Present Simple / Present Cont.	Past Continuous	Past Simple	Future	Conditional	Present Perfect
I	scream – am screaming	was screaming	screamed	will scream	would scream	have screamed
You	scream – are screaming	were screaming	screamed	will scream	would scream	have screamed
He She It	screams – is screaming	was screaming	screamed	will scream	would scream	has screamed
We	scream – are screaming	were screaming	screamed	will scream	would scream	have screamed
You (pl)	scream – are screaming	were screaming	screamed	will scream	would scream	have screamed
They	scream – are screaming	were screaming	screamed	will scream	would scream	have screamed

When Verbita screams , the whole galaxy shakes.

If I stung you, you would scream again.

I screamed so hard at him his ears lit up.

search

Sub.	Present Simple Present Cont.	Past Continuous	Past Simple	Future	Conditional	Present Perfect
I	search – am searching	was searching	searched	will search	would search	have searched
You	search – are searching	were searching	searched	will search	would search	have searched
He She It	searches – is searching	was searching	searched	will search	would search	has searched
We	search – are searching	were searching	searched	will search	would search	have searched
You (pl)	search – are searching	were searching	searched	will search	would search	have searched
They	search – are searching	were searching	searched	will search	would search	have searched

We **are searching** for him day and night.

I **will search** inside this dark warehouse.

They **have searched** high and low.

see

be seen

Sub.	Present Simple / Present Cont.	Past Continuous	Past Simple	Future	Conditional	Present Perfect
I	see – am seeing	was seeing	saw	will see	would see	have seen
You	see – are seeing	were seeing	saw	will see	would see	have seen
He She It	sees – is seeing	was seeing	saw	will see	would see	has seen
We	see – are seeing	were seeing	saw	will see	would see	have seen
You (pl)	see – are seeing	were seeing	saw	will see	would see	have seen
They	see – are seeing	were seeing	saw	will see	would see	have seen

I see strange things ahead of me through my binoculars.

We have seen nothing like this before.

You saw it with your own two eyes.

andyGARNICA

Sub.	Present Simple Present Cont.	Past Continuous	Past Simple	Future	Conditional	Present Perfect
I	separate – am separating	was separating	separated	will separate	would separate	have separated
You	separate – are separating	were separating	separated	will separate	would separate	have separated
He She It	separates is separating	was separating	separated	will separate	would separate	has separated
We	separate – are separating	were separating	separated	will separate	would separate	have separated
You (pl)	separate – are separating	were separating	separated	will separate	would separate	have separated
They	separate – are separating	were separating	separated	will separate	would separate	have separated

This device **separates** the yellow from the blue.

We **have separated** the colo(u)rs successfully.

For my next trick, I **will separate** the red from the green.

show

showing

be shown

show!

andyGARNICA

Sub.	Present Simple / Present Cont.	Past Continuous	Past Simple	Future	Conditional	Present Perfect
I	show – am showing	was showing	showed	will show	would show	have shown/ showed
You	show – are showing	were showing	showed	will show	would show	have shown/ showed
He She It	shows – is showing	was showing	showed	will show	would show	has shown/ showed
We	show – are showing	were showing	showed	will show	would show	have shown/ showed
You (pl)	show – are showing	were showing	showed	will show	would show	have shown/ showed
They	show – are showing	were showing	showed	will show	would show	have shown/ showed

I **am showing** you my new best friend.

Next, he **will show** her his cat, guinea pig, and two hamsters.

You **have shown** me enough for one day, Verbito!

andyGARNICA

Sub.	Present Simple Present Cont.	Past Continuous	Past Simple	Future	Conditional	Present Perfect
I	shower – am showering	was showering	showered	will shower	would shower	have showered
You	shower – are showering	were showering	showered	will shower	would shower	have showered
He She It	showers – is showering	was showering	showered	will shower	would shower	has showered
We	shower – are showering	were showering	showered	will shower	would shower	have showered
You (pl)	shower – are showering	were showering	showered	will shower	would shower	have showered
They	shower – are showering	were showering	showered	will shower	would shower	have showered

I wonder if you **are showering** for the first time, Cyberdog!

I **showered** to get rid of the mud.

We dogs **would shower** even less if we were cats.

79

be sung

sing!

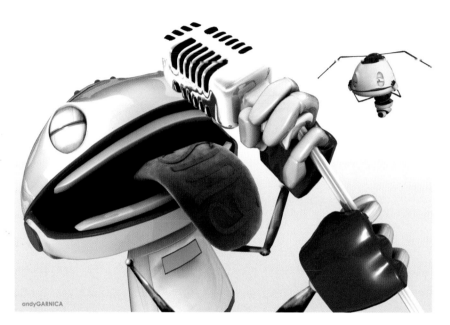

Sub.	Present Simple / Present Cont.	Past Continuous	Past Simple	Future	Conditional	Present Perfect
I	sing — am singing	was singing	sang	will sing	would sing	have sung
You	sing — are singing	were singing	sang	will sing	would sing	have sung
He She It	sings — is singing	was singing	sang	will sing	would sing	has sung
We	sing — are singing	were singing	sang	will sing	would sing	have sung
You (pl)	sing — are singing	were singing	sang	will sing	would sing	have sung
They	sing — are singing	were singing	sang	will sing	would sing	have sung

My family is gifted, and we all sing.

Wow! You sang this with Pink Floyd?

I was singing in bars before I became a star.

Sub.	Present Simple Present Cont.	Past Continuous	Past Simple	Future	Conditional	Present Perfect
I	sit down – am sitting down	was sitting down	sat down	will sit down	would sit down	have sat down
You	sit down – are sitting down	were sitting down	sat down	will sit down	would sit down	have sat down
He She It	sits down – is sitting down	was sitting down	sat down	will sit down	would sit down	has sat down
We	sit down – are sitting down	were sitting down	sat down	will sit down	would sit down	have sat down
You (pl)	sit down – are sitting down	were sitting down	sat down	will sit down	would sit down	have sat down
They	sit down – are sitting down	were sitting down	sat down	will sit down	would sit down	have sat down

He **is sitting down** on his high chair.

They **will sit down** before they get started.

We **would sit down**, but there's only one chair.

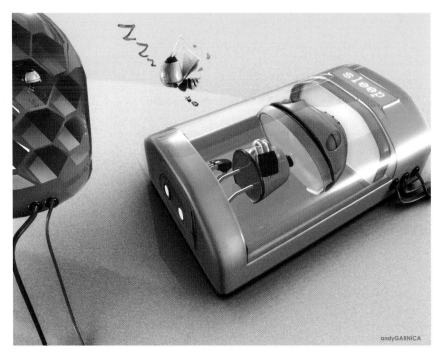

Sub.	Present Simple / Present Cont.	Past Continuous	Past Simple	Future	Conditional	Present Perfect
I	sleep – am sleeping	was sleeping	slept	will sleep	would sleep	have slept
You	sleep – are sleeping	were sleeping	slept	will sleep	would sleep	have slept
He She It	sleeps – is sleeping	was sleeping	slept	will sleep	would sleep	has slept
We	sleep – are sleeping	were sleeping	slept	will sleep	would sleep	have slept
You (pl)	sleep – are sleeping	were sleeping	slept	will sleep	would sleep	have slept
They	sleep – are sleeping	were sleeping	slept	will sleep	would sleep	have slept

We **sleep** in beds that look like metal boxes.

He **will sleep** soundly through the night.

I **would sleep** on my side, but the box is too small.

Sub.	Present Simple / Present Cont.	Past Continuous	Past Simple	Future	Conditional	Present Perfect
I	start – am starting	was starting	started	will start	would start	have started
You	start – are starting	were starting	started	will start	would start	have started
He She It	starts – is starting	was starting	started	will start	would start	has started
We	start – are starting	were starting	started	will start	would start	have started
You (pl)	start – are starting	were starting	started	will start	would start	have started
They	start – are starting	were starting	started	will start	would start	have started

Every time Verbito starts , I end up losing.

I have started panting hard, which usually means I'm about to lose.

Keep trying, Cyberdog, and one day you will start winning!

stop

stopping

stop!

Sub.	Present Simple / Present Cont.	Past Continuous	Past Simple	Future	Conditional	Present Perfect
I	stop – am stopping	was stopping	stopped	will stop	would stop	have stopped
You	stop – are stopping	were stopping	stopped	will stop	would stop	have stopped
He She It	stops – is stopping	was stopping	stopped	will stop	would stop	has stopped
We	stop – are stopping	were stopping	stopped	will stop	would stop	have stopped
You (pl)	stop – are stopping	were stopping	stopped	will stop	would stop	have stopped
They	stop – are stopping	were stopping	stopped	will stop	would stop	have stopped

Everyone **is stopping** at the last possible nanosecond.

I think you **stopped** just in time.

If I were you, I **would stop** sooner.

Sub.	Present Simple / Present Cont.	Past Continuous	Past Simple	Future	Conditional	Present Perfect
I	stroll – am strolling	was strolling	strolled	will stroll	would stroll	have strolled
You	stroll – are strolling	were strolling	strolled	will stroll	would stroll	have strolled
He She It	strolls – is strolling	was strolling	strolled	will stroll	would stroll	has strolled
We	stroll – are strolling	were strolling	strolled	will stroll	would stroll	have strolled
You (pl)	stroll – are strolling	were strolling	strolled	will stroll	would stroll	have strolled
They	stroll – are strolling	were strolling	strolled	will stroll	would stroll	have strolled

I **am strolling** in the early evening.

We **have strolled** along the same stretch every evening this week.

You **were strolling** here yesterday when the other dogs chased you.

andyGARNICA

Sub.	Present Simple / Present Cont.	Past Continuous	Past Simple	Future	Conditional	Present Perfect
I	study – am studying	was studying	studied	will study	would study	have studied
You	study – are studying	were studying	studied	will study	would study	have studied
He She It	studies – is studying	was studying	studied	will study	would study	has studied
We	study – are studying	were studying	studied	will study	would study	have studied
You (pl)	study – are studying	were studying	studied	will study	would study	have studied
They	study – are studying	were studying	studied	will study	would study	have studied

Verbito and a Beebot **are studying** at home.

I **will study** tonight for tomorrow's test.

We **have studied** only when we've had to.

Sub.	Present Simple Present Cont.	Past Continuous	Past Simple	Future	Conditional	Present Perfect
I	swim – am swimming	was swimming	swam	will swim	would swim	have swum
You	swim – are swimming	were swimming	swam	will swim	would swim	have swum
He She It	swims – is swimming	was swimming	swam	will swim	would swim	has swum
We	swim – are swimming	were swimming	swam	will swim	would swim	have swum
You (pl)	swim – are swimming	were swimming	swam	will swim	would swim	have swum
They	swim – are swimming	were swimming	swam	will swim	would swim	have swum

Fish **are swimming** all around me.

I **would swim** faster if I had my fins.

You **will swim** daily on this vacation.

Sub.	Present Simple Present Cont.	Past Continuous	Past Simple	Future	Conditional	Present Perfect
I	talk – am talking	was talking	talked	will talk	would talk	have talked
You	talk – are talking	were talking	talked	will talk	would talk	have talked
He She It	talks – is talking	was talking	talked	will talk	would talk	has talked
We	talk – are talking	were talking	talked	will talk	would talk	have talked
You (pl)	talk – are talking	were talking	talked	will talk	would talk	have talked
They	talk – are talking	were talking	talked	will talk	would talk	have talked

I amaze my audience when I talk.

You will talk a lot on this ten-state tour.

We were talking about your hat, Verbito.

andyGARNICA

Sub.	Present Simple / Present Cont.	Past Continuous	Past Simple	Future	Conditional	Present Perfect
I	test – am testing	was testing	tested	will test	would test	have tested
You	test – are testing	were testing	tested	will test	would test	have tested
He She It	tests – is testing	was testing	tested	will test	would test	has tested
We	test – are testing	were testing	tested	will test	would test	have tested
You (pl)	test – are testing	were testing	tested	will test	would test	have tested
They	test – are testing	were testing	tested	will test	would test	have tested

We **are testing** this machine together.

You **were testing** to see if it produces a shock.

I **have tested** it on Cyberdog, and it seems to work.

think

be thought

thinking
think!

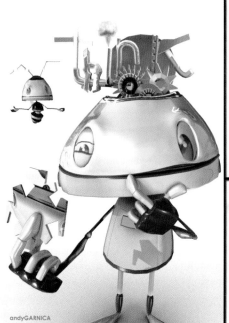

andyGARNICA

Sub.	Present Simple Present Cont.	Past Continuous	Past Simple	Future	Conditional	Present Perfect
I	think – am thinking	was thinking	thought	will think	would think	have thought
You	think – are thinking	were thinking	thought	will think	would think	have thought
He She It	thinks – is thinking	was thinking	thought	will think	would think	has thought
We	think – are thinking	were thinking	thought	will think	would think	have thought
You (pl)	think – are thinking	were thinking	thought	will think	would think	have thought
They	think – are thinking	were thinking	thought	will think	would think	have thought

He **thinks** it fits right here.

I **have thought** about what to do with it.

You **thought** about it long and hard.

90

travel!

andyGARNICA

Sub.	Present Simple Present Cont.	Past Continuous	Past Simple	Future	Conditional	Present Perfect
I	travel – am travel(l)ing	was travel(l)ing	travel(l)ed	will travel	would travel	have travel(l)ed
You	travel – are travel(l)ing	were travel(l)ing	travel(l)ed	will travel	would travel	have travel(l)ed
He She It	travels – is travel(l)ing	was travel(l)ing	travel(l)ed	will travel	would travel	has travel(l)ed
We	travel – are travel(l)ing	were travel(l)ing	travel(l)ed	will travel	would travel	have travel(l)ed
You (pl)	travel – are travel(l)ing	were travel(l)ing	travel(l)ed	will travel	would travel	have travel(l)ed
They	travel – are travel(l)ing	were travel(l)ing	travel(l)ed	will travel	would travel	have travel(l)ed

Verbito **travels** from planet to planet.

You **will travel** to a new planet today.

We **travel(l)ed** far and wide before we arrived here.

andyGARNICA

Sub.	Present Simple / Present Cont.	Past Continuous	Past Simple	Future	Conditional	Present Perfect
I	trip – am tripping	was tripping	tripped	will trip	would trip	have tripped
You	trip – are tripping	were tripping	tripped	will trip	would trip	have tripped
He She It	trips – is tripping	was tripping	tripped	will trip	would trip	has tripped
We	trip – are tripping	were tripping	tripped	will trip	would trip	have tripped
You (pl)	trip – are tripping	were tripping	tripped	will trip	would trip	have tripped
They	trip – are tripping	were tripping	tripped	will trip	would trip	have tripped

I **trip** over the same wire every time.

He **tripped** and fell and was not amused.

You **will trip** if you don't watch out.

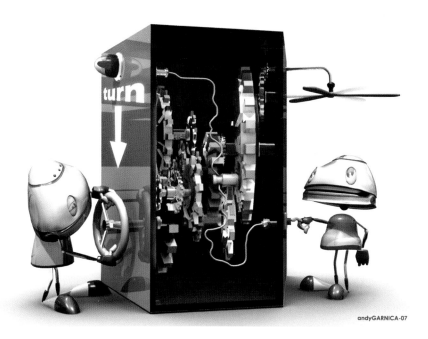

andyGARNICA-07

Sub.	Present Simple / Present Cont.	Past Continuous	Past Simple	Future	Conditional	Present Perfect
I	turn / – / am turning	was turning	turned	will turn	would turn	have turned
You	turn / – / are turning	were turning	turned	will turn	would turn	have turned
He She It	turns / is turning	was turning	turned	will turn	would turn	has turned
We	turn / – / are turning	were turning	turned	will turn	would turn	have turned
You (pl)	turn / – / are turning	were turning	turned	will turn	would turn	have turned
They	turn / – / are turning	were turning	turned	will turn	would turn	have turned

First a wheel **turns**, and then the engine roars.

The wheels **will turn** and the mechanism will spring into action.

He loved it when the fan blades **were turning**.

Sub.	Present Simple Present Cont.	Past Continuous	Past Simple	Future	Conditional	Present Perfect
I	wait – am waiting	was waiting	waited	will wait	would wait	have waited
You	wait – are waiting	were waiting	waited	will wait	would wait	have waited
He She It	waits is waiting	was waiting	waited	will wait	would wait	has waited
We	wait – are waiting	were waiting	waited	will wait	would wait	have waited
You (pl)	wait – are waiting	were waiting	waited	will wait	would wait	have waited
They	wait – are waiting	were waiting	waited	will wait	would wait	have waited

Verbito **waits** patiently at the corner.

We think you **have waited** enough.

I **would wait** a little longer, but I'll miss the beginning of the movie.

waking up
wake up!

wake up
be woken up

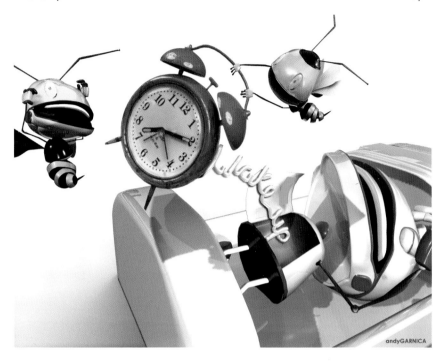

Sub.	Present Simple Present Cont.	Past Continuous	Past Simple	Future	Conditional	Present Perfect
I	wake up – am waking up	was waking up	woke up	will wake up	would wake up	have woken up
You	wake up – are waking up	were waking up	woke up	will wake up	would wake up	have woken up
He She It	wakes up – is waking up	was waking up	woke up	will wake up	would wake up	has woken up
We	wake up – are waking up	were waking up	woke up	will wake up	would wake up	have woken up
You (pl)	wake up – are waking up	were waking up	woke up	will wake up	would wake up	have woken up
They	wake up – are waking up	were waking up	woke up	will wake up	would wake up	have woken up

You wake up at ten past seven every morning.

I have woken up, and it's time for breakfast.

He will wake up earlier tomorrow because he's going to another planet.

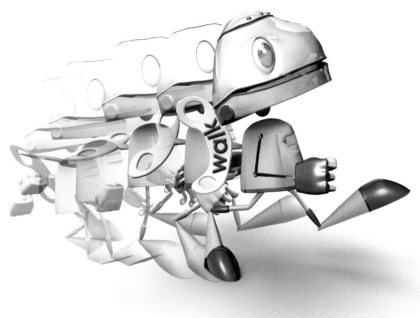

andyGARNICA

Sub.	Present Simple / Present Cont.	Past Continuous	Past Simple	Future	Conditional	Present Perfect
I	walk / – / am walking	was walking	walked	will walk	would walk	have walked
You	walk / – / are walking	were walking	walked	will walk	would walk	have walked
He She It	walks / is walking	was walking	walked	will walk	would walk	has walked
We	walk / – / are walking	were walking	walked	will walk	would walk	have walked
You (pl)	walk / – / are walking	were walking	walked	will walk	would walk	have walked
They	walk / – / are walking	were walking	walked	will walk	would walk	have walked

I **walk** for a mile after eating dinner.

He **would walk** funny if his battery were low.

You **walked** home after the party.

andyGARNICA

Sub.	Present Simple Present Cont.	Past Continuous	Past Simple	Future	Conditional	Present Perfect
I	want – am wanting	was wanting	wanted	will want	would want	have wanted
You	want – are wanting	were wanting	wanted	will want	would want	have wanted
He She It	wants – is wanting	was wanting	wanted	will want	would want	has wanted
We	want – are wanting	were wanting	wanted	will want	would want	have wanted
You (pl)	want – are wanting	were wanting	wanted	will want	would want	have wanted
They	want – are wanting	were wanting	wanted	will want	would want	have wanted

Verbito-boy usually knows what he wants .

I have wanted a Cyberdog all my life!

You wanted to buy it regardless of cost.

97

andyGARNICA

Sub.	Present Simple / Present Cont.	Past Continuous	Past Simple	Future	Conditional	Present Perfect
I	watch – am watching	was watching	watched	will watch	would watch	have watched
You	watch – are watching	were watching	watched	will watch	would watch	have watched
He She It	watches – is watching	was watching	watched	will watch	would watch	has watched
We	watch – are watching	were watching	watched	will watch	would watch	have watched
You (pl)	watch – are watching	were watching	watched	will watch	would watch	have watched
They	watch – are watching	were watching	watched	will watch	would watch	have watched

We **watch** all exits and doors from this room.

You **have watched** these screens throughout your shift.

I **will watch** closely to spot anything suspicious.

98

Sub.	Present Simple Present Cont.	Past Continuous	Past Simple	Future	Conditional	Present Perfect
I	wave – am waving	was waving	waved	will wave	would wave	have waved
You	wave – are waving	were waving	waved	will wave	would wave	have waved
He She It	waves – is waving	was waving	waved	will wave	would wave	has waved
We	wave – are waving	were waving	waved	will wave	would wave	have waved
You (pl)	wave – are waving	were waving	waved	will wave	would wave	have waved
They	wave – are waving	were waving	waved	will wave	would wave	have waved

He **waves** at the gathering of his adoring fans.

The hysterical crowd **waved** and screamed.

I **have waved** so much today my arms ache.

andyGARNICA

Sub.	Present Simple Present Cont.	Past Continuous	Past Simple	Future	Conditional	Present Perfect
I	win – am winning	was winning	won	will win	would win	have won
You	win – are winning	were winning	won	will win	would win	have won
He She It	wins – is winning	was winning	won	will win	would win	has won
We	win – are winning	were winning	won	will win	would win	have won
You (pl)	win – are winning	were winning	won	will win	would win	have won
They	win – are winning	were winning	won	will win	would win	have won

He always **wins** because his aunt runs the selection committee.

I **have won** the "Robot of the Year" award twice in a row.

Do you think you **will win** again next year, Verbito?

write

andyGARNICA

Sub.	Present Simple / Present Cont.	Past Continuous	Past Simple	Future	Conditional	Present Perfect
I	write – am writing	was writing	wrote	will write	would write	have written
You	write – are writing	were writing	wrote	will write	would write	have written
He She It	writes – is writing	was writing	wrote	will write	would write	has written
We	write – are writing	were writing	wrote	will write	would write	have written
You (pl)	write – are writing	were writing	wrote	will write	would write	have written
They	write – are writing	were writing	wrote	will write	would write	have written

He **writes** essays on his computer that no one ever reads.

One day I **will write** my memoirs.

We **wrote** a short note to the chief robot.

Verb Index

This index combines three features:

- All 101 conjugated verbs appear in **bold**, cross-referenced to their **page numbers**.
- Common phrasal verb forms of the 101 model verbs are listed under the main verb (followed by an explanation of each meaning in parentheses).
- An additional fifty common irregular verbs are included with their principal parts.

All irregular verbs are shown with following forms:

present simple • third person singular • present participle • past simple • past participle

The principal parts of regular verbs (to ———, ——— (e)s, ———ing, ——— (e)d, ——— (e)d) are not shown.

be **able to** • is able to • being able to • was/were able to • been able to **1**
arise • arises • arising • arose • arisen
arrest 2
arrive 3
   arrive at *(reach a place or decision)*
ask
   ask about *(inquire about)*
   ask after *(inquire about someone's well-being)*
   ask for *(request)* **4**
   ask for it *(deserve or provoke something negative happening)*
be • is • being • was/were • been **5**
bear • bears • bearing • bore • borne
beat • beats • beating • beat • beaten
begin • begins • beginning • began • begun
bite • bites • biting • bit • bitten
blow • blows • blowing • blew • blown
break • breaks • breaking • broke • broken
bring • brings • bringing • brought • brought **6**
   bring about *(cause a particular outcome)*
   bring on *(encourage development)*
   bring up *(raise a subject for discussion)*
build • builds • building • built • built **7**
buy • buys • buying • bought • bought **8**
   buy into *(buy partial ownership of; accept an idea or proposal)*
   buy out *(purchase someone's entire stake in something)*
   buy up *(purchase a lot of)*
call 9
   call (a)round *(telephone people in succession)*
   call by *(visit)*

call for *(demand or request)*
call off *(cancel)*
call on *(visit; request of someone)*
call over *(beckon to come here)*
call up *(telephone)*

carry 10
carry off *(take away; accomplish)*
carry out *(implement a plan)*

catch • catches • catching • caught • caught

change 11
change into *(transform into; change one's clothing for)*
change over to *(convert to)*

choose • chooses • choosing • chose • chosen

clean 12
clean out *(tidy by ridding of unwanted things)*
clean up *(tidy or organize)*

close 13
close off *(close entirely)*
close up *(shut)*

comb 14

come • comes • coming • came • come **15**
come by *(visit casually)*
come into *(enter; gain, such as with inheritance money)*
come off *(detach; happen successfully)*
come on *(hurry; start working)*
come over *(appear to others; visit)*
come through *(survive; endure)*
come to *(add up to; make of oneself; reach)*

cook 16
cook up *(prepare an amount of food; invent an idea or plan)*

cost • costs • costing • cost/costed • cost

count 17
count off *(tally)*
count up *(add to a total)*

crash 18
crash into *(collide with)*

create 19

cut • cuts • cutting • cut • cut **20**
cut along *(cut by following a line)*
cut into *(slice into)*
cut off *(detach by cutting)*
cut through *(slice through)*
cut up *(cut into pieces)*

dance 21
dance around *(avoid an issue or problem)*

decide 22
decide for *(make a decision in favo[u]r of)*
decide on *(make a decision about)*

dig • digs • digging • dug • dug

direct 23

do • does • doing • did • done

draw • draws • drawing • drew • drawn
dream • dreams • dreaming • dreamed/dreamt • dreamed/dreamt   **24**
    dream about *(picture in one's sleep or fantasy)*
    dream of *(imagine; conceive)*
    dream up *(invent)*
get **dressed** • gets dressed • getting dressed • got(ten) dressed • got(ten) dressed   **25**
drink • drinks • drinking • drank • drunk   **26**
    drink up *(drink all of)*
drive • drives • driving • drove • driven   **27**
    drive at *(allude to; suggest)*
eat • eats • eating • ate • eaten   **28**
    eat in *(eat a meal at home)*
    eat out *(dine away from home)*
    eat up *(complete eating all of)*
    overeat *(eat to excess)*
enter   **29**
    enter into *(take part in; enrol[l])*
fall • falls • falling • fell • fallen   **30**
    fall for *(develop romantic feelings toward)*
    fall off *(decline; drop from something)*
    fall through *(fail [of a plan])*
    fall (up)on *(be dependent on; encounter; attack)*
feed • feeds • feeding • fed • fed
feel • feels • feeling • felt • felt
fight • fights • fighting • fought • fought   **31**
    fight over *(battle with someone else for control or ownership of)*
    fight through *(successfully make one's way through a situation)*
find • finds • finding • found • found   **32**
    find out *(discover)*
    find out about *(uncover the truth about)*
finish   **33**
    finish off *(complete; kill)*
    finish up *(conclude one's business)*
fly • flies • flying • flew • flown
follow   **34**
    follow through *(manage until a conclusion is reached)*
    follow up *(check on; ensure something was done)*
forbid • forbids • forbidding • forbade • forbidden   **35**
forget • forgets • forgetting • forgot • forgotten   **36**
    forget about *(no longer remember something)*
freeze • freezes • freezing • froze • frozen
get • gets • getting • got/gotten • got/gotten
give • gives • giving • gave • given   **37**
    give back *(return; surrender; admit defeat)*
    give out *(distribute)*
    give up *(stop doing something in failure)*
go • goes • going • went • gone   **38**
    go along with *(accept)*
    go (a)round *(circumnavigate; reach one's aim by avoiding something)*
    go down *(descend; decrease; decline)*   **39**
    go out *(exit; extinguish [of a light, candle])*   **40**

go through *(proceed from one side to the other; endure)*
go under *(fail financially)*
go up *(increase; approach)*
grow • grows • growing • grew • grown **41**
    grow into *(develop into)*
    grow up *(become more mature)*
hang • hangs • hanging • hanged/hung • hanged/hung
have • has • having • had • had **42**
    have against *(bear a grudge against)*
    have around *(invite to visit; possess)*
    have on *(be wearing)*
hear • hears • hearing • heard • heard **43**
    hear about *(learn about)*
    hear from *(get a message from)*
    hear of *(learn about the existence of)*
hide • hides • hiding • hid • hidden
hit • hits • hitting • hit • hit
hold • holds • holding • held • held
jump **44**
    jump down *(leap in a downward motion)*
    jump in *(decisively involve oneself in the situation)*
    jump over *(leap over the top of)*
    jump up *(leap upward; suddenly appear)*
keep • keeps • keeping • kept • kept
kick **45**
    kick off *(start)*
    kick over *(knock down)*
kiss **46**
    kiss up *(try to gain favo[u]r by praise)*
kneel • kneels • kneeling • knelt/kneeled • knelt/kneeled
know • knows • knowing • knew • known **47**
    know about *(be aware of)*
    know of *(be aware of the existence of)*
leap • leaps • leaping • leapt/leaped • leapt/leaped
learn • learns • learning • learned/learnt • learned/learnt **48**
    learn about *(discover)*
    learn of *(discover by chance)*
    learn through *(find out by means of)*
leave • leaves • leaving • left • left
lend • lends • lending • lent • lent
let • lets • letting • let • let
lie • lies • lying • lay • laid
lie (tell a) • lies • lying • lied • lied **49**
    lie about *(tell an untruth about)*
light • lights • lighting • lit • lit **50**
    light up *(start to shine; illuminate)*
like **51**
live **52**
lose • loses • losing • lost • lost **53**
    lose out *(end up at a disadvantage in a situation)*
love **54**

make • makes • making • made • made   **55**
   make do *(put up with; settle for)*
   make off with *(steal; go away with something)*
   make up *(invent)*
get **married** • gets married • getting married • got(ten) married • got(ten) married
   56
mean • means • meaning • meant • meant
meet • meets • meeting • met • met
open   **57**
   open up *(open wide; reveal one's thoughts or feelings)*
organize   **58**
paint   **59**
   paint over *(cover with paint)*
pay • pays • paying • paid • paid   **60**
   pay in *(put money into)*
   pay off *(settle an account; pay what is owed)*
   pay out *(give winnings or earnings)*
play   **61**
   play along *(pretend to follow)*
   play around *(act foolishly)*
   play at *(pretend to be)*
   play on *(continue playing; exploit)*
   play up *(emphasize; act erratically)*
   play with *(enjoy a game with; toy with)*
polish   **62**
   polish off *(completely finish; eat entirely)*
put • puts • putting • put • put   **63**
   put by *(set aside)*
   put off *(postpone)*
be **quiet** • is quiet • being quiet • was/were quiet • been quiet   **64**
quit   **65**
rain   **66**
   rain down (on) *(rain heavily; occur in large numbers or amount)*
read • reads • reading • read • read   **67**
   read between the lines *(understand the hidden message)*
   read over *(look through)*
   read through *(read from start to finish)*
   read up on *(research)*
receive   **68**
record   **69**
remember   **70**
repair   **71**
return   **72**
   return for *(come back to retrieve)*
   return to *(come back to)*
ride • rides • riding • rode • ridden
ring • rings • ringing • rang • rung
rise • rises • rising • rose • risen
run • runs • running • ran • run   **73**
   run around *(be busy in activity)*
   run by *(briefly bring some information or idea to someone's notice for approval;
      stop by someplace quickly)*

run into *(meet by chance)*
run over *(knock down)*
say • says • saying • said • said
scream   74
scream at *(shout very loudly at)*
scream for *(demand by yelling)*
search   75
search for *(look for)*
search out *(seek and find)*
see • sees • seeing • saw • seen   **76**
see in *(appreciate a quality)*
see off *(successfully deter or reject; accompany to departure)*
see through *(be able to; realize someone's real aim)*
seem • seems • seeming • seemed • seemed
sell • sells • selling • sold • sold
send • sends • sending • sent • sent
separate   77
shine • shines • shining • shone • shone
show • shows • showing • showed • shown   **78**
show off *(display ostentatiously)*
show through *(be visible through something)*
show up *(appear; highlight failings)*
shower   79
sing • sings • singing • sang • sung   **80**
sit down • sits down • sitting down • sat down • sat down   **81**
sleep • sleeps • sleeping • slept • slept   **82**
sleep over *(stay the night at someone's house)*
sleep through *(remain asleep for the duration)*
spend • spends • spending • spent • spent
spill • spills • spilling • spilled/spilt • spilled/spilt
spin • spins • spinning • span • spun
spit • spits • spitting • spat • spat
stand • stands • standing • stood • stood
start   83
start off *(begin)*
start up *(begin [especially an engine, a company, a discussion])*
steal • steals • stealing • stole • stolen
stick • sticks • sticking • stuck • stuck
stop   84
stop by *(halt momentarily at)*
stop off at *(halt one's journey at)*
stop up *(clog)*
stroll   85
stroll by *(walk past)*
stroll into *(walk casually into)*
study   86
study under *(be taught by a particular professor or other expert)*
swim • swims • swimming • swam • swum   **87**
take • takes • taking • took • taken
talk   88
talk about *(discuss a subject)*
talk of *(discuss)*

talk through *(lead through by talking)*

talk up *(exaggerate)*

teach • teaches • teaching • taught • taught

tear • tears • tearing • tore • torn

tell • tells • telling • told • told

(tell a) lie • tells a lie • telling a lie • told a lie • told a lie **49**

test 89

test for *(conduct tests to determine the presence of something)*

think • thinks • thinking • thought • thought **90**

think of *(come to mind)*

think through *(mentally analyze the consequences)*

throw • throws • throwing • threw • thrown

travel 91

travel (a)round *(journey to different places)*

trip 92

trip over *(stumble and fall)*

trip up *(fall; make a mistake; make someone fail)*

turn 93

turn (a)round *(move in the opposite direction)*

turn off *(switch off; deter)*

turn on *(switch on; arouse)*

turn over *(flip)*

turn up *(appear)*

understand • understands • understanding • understood • understood

undo • undoes • undoing • undid • undone

wait 94

wait on *(attend to someone's needs)*

wait out *(endure until the end)*

wake • wakes • waking • woke • woken

wake up • wakes up • waking up • woke up • woken up **95**

walk 96

walk away *(depart; avoid becoming involved in)*

walk off *(leave the scene)*

walk over *(treat badly)*

want 97

want for *(lack)*

watch 98

watch out *(keep alert to)*

wave 99

wear • wears • wearing • wore • worn

win • wins • winning • won • won **100**

win (a)round *(persuade to one's point of view)*

win over *(persuade to one's point of view)*

write • writes • writing • wrote • written **101**

write off *(consider not worth saving)*

write up *(write a report on)*

The Passive Construction

infinitive: to find

passive infinitive: to be found

Sub.	Present Simple / Present Cont.	Past Continuous	Past Simple	Future	Conditional	Present Perfect
I	am / am being	was being	was	will be	would be	have been
You	are / are being	were being	were	will be	would be	have been
He / She / It	is / is being	was being	was	will be	would be	has been
We	are / are being	were being	were	will be	would be	have been
You (pl)	are / are being	were being	were	will be	would be	have been
They	are / are being	were being	were	will be	would be	have been

found

Regular Verb Conjugation

infinitive: to cook

phrasal verb: to cook **up**

gerund: cooking

command: cook!

Present	Present Simple			Present Continuous			
	I	cook	-	I	am	cook	ing
	You	cook	-	You	are	cook	ing
	He/She/It	cook	s	He/She/It	is	cook	ing
	We	cook	-	We	are	cook	ing
	You	cook	-	You	are	cook	ing
	They	cook	-	They	are	cook	ing

Past Continuous			
I	was	cook	ing
You	were	cook	ing
He/She/It	was	cook	ing
We	were	cook	ing
You	were	cook	ing
They	were	cook	ing

Past Simple		
I	cook	ed
You	cook	ed
He/She/It	cook	ed
We	cook	ed
You	cook	ed
They	cook	ed

Future		
I	will	cook
You	will	cook
He/She/It	will	cook
We	will	cook
You	will	cook
They	will	cook

Conditional		
I	would	cook
You	would	cook
He/She/It	would	cook
We	would	cook
You	would	cook
They	would	cook

Present Perfect			
I	have	cook	ed
You	have	cook	ed
He/She/It	has	cook	ed
We	have	cook	ed
You	have	cook	ed
They	have	cook	ed